CATS AND DOGS

Amanda O'Neill

KING*f*ISHER

CONTENTS

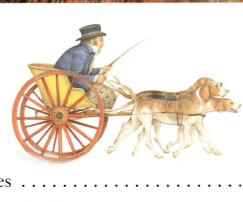

DOGS
Dog family 4
The first dogs 6
Wild dogs today 8
From wolf to pet 10

DOG DESIGN
A dog's body 12
Appearances count . .14

Senses 16
Puppy development 18

DOGS AND PEOPLE
Hunting dogs 20
The nose that knows 22
Herding dogs 24
Beware of the dog 26
Guides and helpers 28
The lap of luxury 30
Dog mythology 32
Magical dogs 34

YOU AND YOUR DOG
Choosing a dog 36
Canine care 38
Dog language 40
The well-trained dog 42
Breeds of dog 44

KINGFISHER
Kingfisher Publications Plc
New Penderel House, 283–288 High Holborn,
London WC1V 7HZ
www.kingfisherpub.com

Material in this edition previously published by Kingfisher
Publications Plc in the *Best-Ever* series

This edition published by Kingfisher Publications Plc 2001
10 9 8 7 6 5 4 3 2 1

1TR/0501/TWP/UNIV(MAR)/150SIN

Copyright © Kingfisher Publications Plc 1998, 1999

All rights reserved. No part of this publication may
be reproduced, stored in a retrieval system or transmitted
by any means, electronic, mechanical, photocopying or
otherwise, without the prior permission of the publisher.

A CIP catalogue record for this book is available from the British
Library.

ISBN 0 7534 0616 0

Printed in Singapore

CATS
Cat family 46
Evolution of the cat 48

CAT DESIGN
The elastic skeleton 50
Balancing tricks 52
Teeth and claws 54
The fur coat 56
Cats' eyes 58
More senses 60
Playtime! 62
Body beautiful 64
Bringing up baby 66

CATS AND PEOPLE
Myth and magic 68
Cats of the East 70
Cats of the West. 72
The longhair story 74
Cat shows 76

YOU AND YOUR CAT
Choosing a cat 78
Cat kit 80
Cat care 82
Understanding your cat. 84
Breeds of cat 86

REFERENCE SECTION
Glossary 88
Famous cats and dogs 91
Index and Acknowledgements 92

DOG FAMILY

Dogs vary in size, shape and appearance more than any other animal species. For example, all cats, whether Siamese or tiger, share a family resemblance. But dog breeds vary so much that it is hard to believe that a Mastiff and a Chihuahua belong to the same species.

How do you choose between giants such as the Irish Wolfhound (1) and the Great Dane (2) or miniatures such as the Chihuahua (3) and the Dachshund (4), or between the shaggy Old English Sheepdog (5) and the naked Mexican Hairless (6)? All of these dogs can make the best of companions, but it is important to choose a breed that will suit your own lifestyle.

For centuries, humans have taken advantage of the dog's adaptable design to develop different types of dog for different jobs, such as hunting, guarding or herding. Today there are dogs with stumpy legs or stilt-like legs, heavy coats or none at all, long noses or flat faces, upright ears or floppy ears. But whatever its type, the dog has a long ancestry as man's best friend.

A Yorkshire Terrier only comes up to the ankles of a Mastiff, which may be more than one hundred times its size.

Officially, the Chihuahua is the smallest breed, but a few Yorkies are smaller than any Chihuahua. Indeed, the record-holder, which lived in the 1940s, was no bigger than a cigarette packet.

The first dogs

Dogs, like cats, bears and other modern carnivores, trace their ancestry back some 60 million years to a small, weasel-like beast called *Miacis*. The dog family began about 20 million years later with *Miacis*' descendant, the mongoose-like *Cynodictus*, to be followed by the first 'nearly dog', *Hesperocyon* or 'Dawn Dog'.

Canine cousins
Near-dogs, such as the jackal-like Dhole and badger-like Raccoon Dog, belong to separate branches of the family from true dogs and wolves.

Bug hunter
In the tropical jungle of what is now North America, *Hesperocyon* hunted insects and small mammals on the forest floor. Short-legged and long-toed, it was still more mongoose than dog.

PALEOCENE PERIOD (65 to 55 million years ago)   **EOCENE PERIOD** (55 to 38 million years ago)   **OLIGOCENE PERIOD** (38 to 25 million years ago)

Bone-crushers
Hyena dogs such as *Osteoborus* were bear-like with bone-crushing teeth. They died out eight million years ago.

Dead ends
Many early members of the canine family, such as the hyena dogs, formed evolutionary dead ends, leaving no descendants.

The earliest pre-dogs were not very dog-like. Scuttling round forest floors or even climbing trees, they had yet to develop the speed to run down prey or the pack-hunting habits of modern dogs. But between seven and five million years ago, the Dawn Dog's descendants evolved into true dogs. Other branches of the family split off to develop into cousins of the modern dog and wolf – including foxes and near-dogs like the Raccoon Dog and Dhole.

Prairie runners
The way opened up for the evolution of true dogs when the spread of open grassland created a space for large, swift grazing animals. To hunt such prey, early dogs began to develop the speed and pack-hunting techniques typical of modern dogs. About one million years ago, the mighty Dire Wolf, now extinct, and our modern Grey Wolf, both evolved.

MIOCENE PERIOD
(25 to 5 million years ago)

PLEISTOCENE PERIOD
(2 million to 10,000 years ago)

HOLOCENE PERIOD
(recent)

Wild dogs today

Our domestic dog is just one member of a large, widespread family, the *Canids*, which includes wild dogs, wolves and foxes. The wolf, once found throughout most of Europe and North America, remains among the best known member of the dog family, but today its range is greatly reduced.

Wolves are family animals, sharing care of cubs and hunting together. Their social nature means that their descendant, the dog, is well adapted to accept a family role among humans.

The wolf used to roam much of the northern part of the world. But destruction of the wolf and its habitat by people mean it is now restricted to the wilderness areas of North America and Asia, some forests of central and eastern Europe and a few hilly areas of countries near the Mediterranean and in the Middle East.

Furry snowsuit
The Arctic Fox is well adapted to life in the frozen north. Its dense coat covers even the soles of its feet – vital protection in its harsh world of ice and snow.

Canine omnivore
Rudyard Kipling called the Golden Jackal 'the belly that runs on four feet', and indeed it eats absolutely anything, from creepy crawlies to fruit and vegetables.

Long legs
Nicknamed 'the fox on stilts', the Maned Wolf is neither fox nor wolf. This South American canine hunts only small prey, from rodents to slugs and snails.

Winter sleeper
The Raccoon Dog is the only member of the dog family to hibernate in winter. A native of the Far East, it has been introduced by man into Eastern Europe.

The dog family can adapt to life almost anywhere, from the Arctic wastes to scorching deserts. Some members, such as the African Hunting Dog, are big, powerful hunters of large prey, while others, such as the Bat-eared Fox, are small insect-eaters. Between them, the 32 wild species have settled every continent except Antarctica (and Australia's only wild dog, the Dingo, was actually brought to Australia centuries ago by primitive man). Today, hunting and, above all, habitat destruction have placed many of the world's wild dogs in danger of extinction.

Living with man
Many of the smaller wild dogs have learned that there are good pickings to be found among human settlements, and the Red Fox is as common in towns as in the country. It even makes its home in the heart of the largest cities. Parks and gardens provide safe den sites, while fox restaurants abound in the form of rubbish dumps, compost heaps, dustbins and bird tables.

In ancient times as now, dogs were children's playmates and guardians. Settlements were vulnerable to attack by animals and human raiders, so fierce dogs were valued for protection.

The dog's sense of family attached it strongly to its owners, as an ever-present companion, not just as a hanger-on. Dogs were also useful rubbish disposers!

It did not take early man long to realise that the dog's hunting skills could be put to good use. Just as a wolf pack hunts co-operatively together, man and dog worked as a team to catch dinner.

From wolf to pet

The dog is not just man's best friend – it is probably our *oldest* friend. Archaeological evidence suggests that the dog was the first animal to be domesticated. Some of the oldest known remains date back to 10,000 BC. But recent studies suggest that pet dogs may have been around much longer, and that three quarters of the dogs alive today trace their ancestry back to a single female wolf who lived 100,000 years ago. So some scientists regard that as the time when wolves joined up with humans and started to become dogs. Today, wolves are rare – while dogs have become a success story.

The starting point of all dogs was the wolf, perhaps tamed by early man once it had moved to within foraging distance of human settlements. Over the years, the descendants of these tame wolves became something different. The key change was one of character rather than looks: the dog is essentially a wolf that never grows up, but remains dependent on its human family. A secondary change was the wide range of shapes and sizes that developed. 'Breeds' such as the Greyhound and Mastiff evolved at least 4,000 years ago.

Hunting partnership
Hunters of the Zande tribe of Central Africa train their Basenji dogs to drive game through the bush towards their nets. Because Basenjis don't bark, bells are put around their neck so that their owners can hear where they are. This method of hunting is thousands of years old, as is the Basenji breed. Ancient Egyptian art from 2300BC shows prick-eared, curly-tailed dogs remarkably like the breed we know today.

Divine dingo
Australia's well-known 'wild dog', the Dingo, is actually a descendant of dogs introduced to the continent by humans, perhaps 4,000 years ago.

In this Aborigine rock painting, the dingo is portrayed as one of the Aborigines' revered ancestors, accompanying the ancestor-spirits of the human race.

Song dog
In the more remote parts of the world, native peoples still keep dogs of very ancient type. The American Indian Dog (nicknamed the 'Song Dog' for its high voice) is a handsome example which closely resembles its wild cousin, the Coyote. Now rare, it was once kept widely by Native Americans from Canada to Mexico.

A DOG'S BODY

 The dog's body is perfectly suited to a hunter's life – strong, swift and equipped with powerful jaws. Although domestic breeds have developed almost every variation of shape and size imaginable, the basic model is still recognisable underneath.

Pug

Bulldog

Mastiff

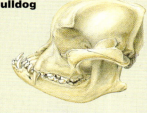
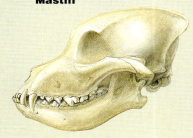

The short legs, flat nose or barrel chest of many specially bred dogs mean they are not as well equipped to survive in the wild as their ancestor, the wolf. Bulldogs, for example, often suffer a range of health problems.

On your marks!
Dogs love to run, but compared with many other running animals they are not among the fastest. The typical dog is built for staying power rather than high speed. A steady, energy-saving trot will carry it for many

Problems ahead
The head shapes of some modern breeds are not always very practical. Shortened skulls, such as the Pug's and Bulldog's, mean misplaced teeth and breathing problems. Compare them with the Mastiff's skull, which is nearer to the wolf's long, strong head.

Legging it
Dogs' legs are designed for long-distance running. The limb bones are usually long, although some specially bred dogs, such as Dachshunds, have been selected for their very short legs.

12

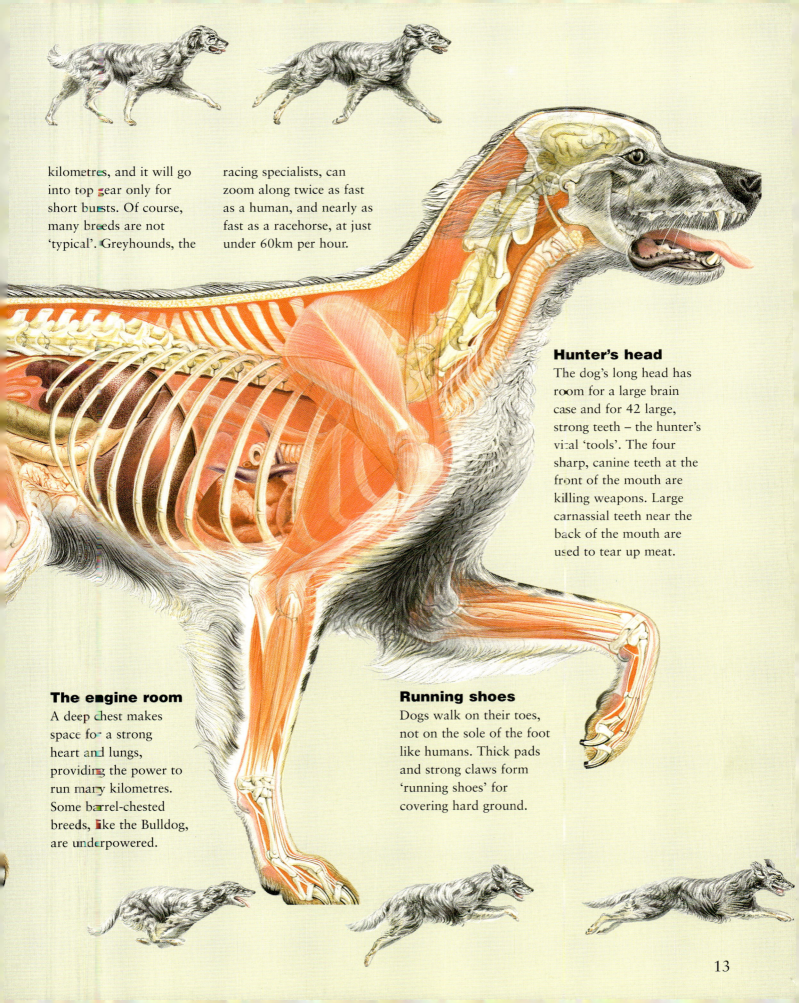

kilometres, and it will go into top gear only for short bursts. Of course, many breeds are not 'typical'. Greyhounds, the racing specialists, can zoom along twice as fast as a human, and nearly as fast as a racehorse, at just under 60km per hour.

Hunter's head
The dog's long head has room for a large brain case and for 42 large, strong teeth – the hunter's vital 'tools'. The four sharp, canine teeth at the front of the mouth are killing weapons. Large carnassial teeth near the back of the mouth are used to tear up meat.

The engine room
A deep chest makes space for a strong heart and lungs, providing the power to run many kilometres. Some barrel-chested breeds, like the Bulldog, are underpowered.

Running shoes
Dogs walk on their toes, not on the sole of the foot like humans. Thick pads and strong claws form 'running shoes' for covering hard ground.

13

Appearances count

A wild dog's fur is a practical all-weather outfit. It protects the skin and keeps out cold and excess heat. It is really two garments in one: a tough top coat of long, strong guard hairs covering an undercoat of short, softer fur. Some breeds wear the same coat as their wild ancestors. Others have developed more 'fashionable' fur – floor-length, crewcut short, curly, wiry or even dreadlocked!

Terrier trims
The thick white coat of the Westie, or West Highland White Terrier, needs care. Compare the different styles of the show dog (1) and the clipped pet (2).

Types of coat
The Dobermann's short, close-lying coat is easy to groom, but others take more work. Rough coats such as the Border Terrier's need stripping or clipping, while the Afghan's flowing locks and the Puli's cords require constant attention.

Dobermann

Afghan Hound

Hungarian Puli

Border Terrier

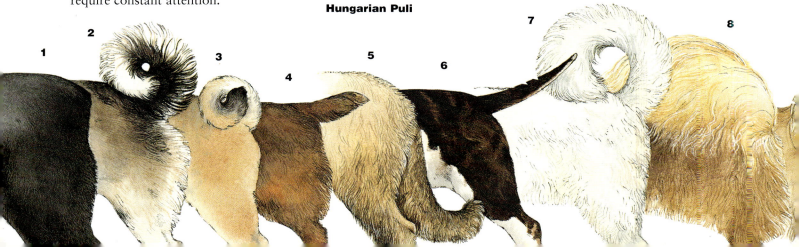

Maxi-coat
The American Cocker has a massive coat, carefully shaped for show dogs (3) and usually clipped for pets (4) for reasons of care and comfort.

Nature designed dogs' ears to stand up in a triangular, funnel shape, which traps and channels sound. But humans have bred dogs with different ear shapes, sizes and positions. For example, all puppies are born with soft ears, which flop down. By selecting dogs whose ears stay babyish all their lives, we have produced drop-eared domestic breeds such as the Basset Hound.

natural ears: wolf

erect ears: German Shepherd Dog

semi-drop ears: Collie

rounded bat-ears: Basenji

drop ears: Basset

pendant ears: Dalmatian

rose ears: Bulldog

button ears: Fox Terrier

Curly-coated Retriever

Shar Pei

The dog's design is adaptable, allowing breeders to develop shapes and styles to suit their fancy. At times they take this too far, breeding coats too heavy for comfort or noses too flat to breathe through. What pleases the human eye may not be good for the dog, so before buying a pup, check if the breed has health problems.

KEY TO TAILS
1 Schipperke (bob tail)
2 Elkhound (single-curled tail)
3 Pug (double-curled tail)
4 Norfolk Terrier (docked tail)
5 Briard (hook tail)
6 Bull Terrier (whip tail)
7 Pyrenean Mountain Dog (plume held high)
8 Pomeranian (plume across back)
9 Pekingese (squirrel tail)
10 Irish Water Spaniel (rat tail)
11 Afghan Hound (ring tail)
12 German Shepherd Dog (sabre tail)
13 Chinese Crested (tufted tail)

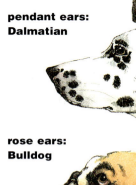

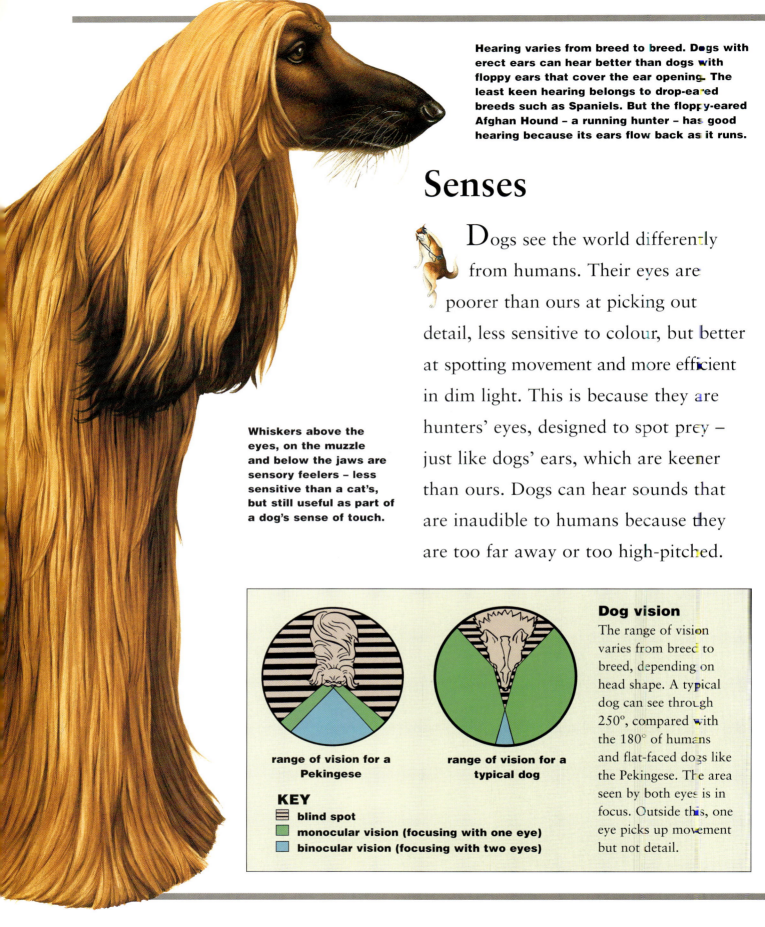

Hearing varies from breed to breed. Dogs with erect ears can hear better than dogs with floppy ears that cover the ear opening. The least keen hearing belongs to drop-eared breeds such as Spaniels. But the floppy-eared Afghan Hound – a running hunter – has good hearing because its ears flow back as it runs.

Senses

Dogs see the world differently from humans. Their eyes are poorer than ours at picking out detail, less sensitive to colour, but better at spotting movement and more efficient in dim light. This is because they are hunters' eyes, designed to spot prey – just like dogs' ears, which are keener than ours. Dogs can hear sounds that are inaudible to humans because they are too far away or too high-pitched.

Whiskers above the eyes, on the muzzle and below the jaws are sensory feelers – less sensitive than a cat's, but still useful as part of a dog's sense of touch.

range of vision for a Pekingese

range of vision for a typical dog

KEY
- blind spot
- monocular vision (focusing with one eye)
- binocular vision (focusing with two eyes)

Dog vision
The range of vision varies from breed to breed, depending on head shape. A typical dog can see through 250°, compared with the 180° of humans and flat-faced dogs like the Pekingese. The area seen by both eyes is in focus. Outside this, one eye picks up movement but not detail.

Termites are the main item on the menu for the Bat-eared Fox. Those huge ears are tuned in to insect footsteps!

A dog uses its keen sense of smell not just for hunting but for checking its surroundings and communicating with other dogs via scent messages. A dog can read the messages in urine and faecal markers, footprints and scent particles carried on the air. Sniffing power varies from breed to breed but, for example, the German Shepherd Dog has 220 million scent cells in its nose – compared to a human's five million.

Smell specialist

Bloodhounds are famed for their keen nose. Like other dogs, they follow both ground scent, made by feet on the ground, and air scent, left hanging in the air after people have gone by. Their sense of smell is so acute they can follow air scent more than a day after the person has gone. The mystery of mass murderer Jack the Ripper might have been solved if police hadn't abandoned plans to set Bloodhounds on his trail.

Secret senses

Scientists haven't cracked all the secrets of a dog's senses. Somehow Rupert the Border Collie is able to sense when his owner is about to have an epileptic fit and warn her in time to move to safety. She can also rely on him to call an ambulance or bring her the cordless telephone.

newborn puppy

A nest of puppies
Baby puppies cuddle up close in their nest to keep warm. By the time they are about a week old, they are strong enough to crawl around the nest, searching for milk and burrowing into their bedding. Eyes and ears begin to open at about two weeks, but it takes another two or three weeks before they work properly. Sleep and food are the pups' only real concerns at this age.

9–14 days old

Newly born
Newborn puppies are completely dependent on their mothers. Their eyes and ears are sealed shut – they do not need them yet. But their noses work from the start, so they can sniff out their milk supply.

Puppy development

For the first two or three weeks of life, puppies do little but sleep and feed. By about three weeks, most pups start to take an interest in life and in each other. When they learn to play, at about four weeks, they are starting their schooling – learning how to be dogs. By about 12 weeks, most puppies are able to join in grown-up activities.

The world around
Once eyes, ears and legs are under control, at about four or five weeks, playtime begins. This is the age when puppies start getting used to the world they will live in as adults. They need to experience normal household noises and activity, and to learn that humans are their friends.

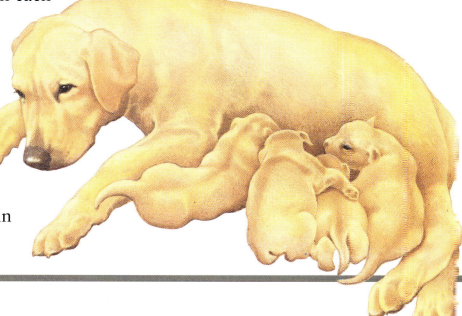

A spotless start

Not all puppies arrive in their adult colours. Yorkshire Terriers are born black, and Dalmatians start out completely spotless. The characteristic spots start to appear when the pups are about two weeks old.

Nursery numbers
The number of puppies born in a litter varies. Small breeds usually have a small litter, perhaps only two or three pups. Large breeds such as the Great Dane can produce more than twenty puppies in a litter. Such huge litters are too much for the mother to feed. If all are to live, some pups must be bottle-fed.

A puppy is ready to leave its first home and go to a new owner somewhere beween six and twelve weeks, depending on the breed. For domestic dogs, it is the key age for a pup to learn about people and attach itself to its new owners.

Mother and pup
The role of the mother is very important in bringing up well-adjusted pups. If she is nervous or snappy, for example, she may pass this on to her offspring.

19

Hunting dogs

Thousands of years ago, humans developed different types of specialist hunting dogs which were faster, stronger or keener-nosed than the original wolf model. They formed two groups – speed specialists (sight hounds) and nose specialists (scent hounds). Hounds are still important today, often as companions rather than hunters.

In the Middle Ages, hunting with hounds was the sport of kings and noblemen. A royal pack might consist of more than a hundred hounds of different kinds. All were known by name and lovingly tended, and the favourites often slept in the king's bed.

Wire-haired Dachshund

Beagle

Saluki

Hounds at home
Today, many hound breeds are popular pets. The Saluki is more favoured as a glamorous companion than as the tough hunter of game, and the Dachshund is so popular as a pet that few realise it began life as a worker, hunting badgers.

20

Foxhounds were bred for speed and hunting ability. Hunters have always loved the 'music' of a pack of hounds baying on the trail, and in the past even picked hounds for the quality of their voices.

In pre-Roman Britain, small hunting dogs were developed to follow prey underground. Known as terriers (from Latin *terra*, meaning 'earth'), their small size and cocky temperament make them great companions.

Made in Britain

Most terriers were bred in Britain, as their names imply – Welsh, Irish, Skye. The Cairn is a Scot, named for the rock heaps it hunted through. Other countries now breed their own, such as Germany's Jagdterrier.

21

The nose that knows

The dog's nose has served humans well in hunting and tracking, but has proved to have more specialist uses. Gundogs (originally falconers' dogs) were developed to sniff out game for hunters. Today, they also play a vital role as sniffer dogs, finding anything from explosives and drugs to lost children and gas leaks.

Monks of the St Bernard's Hospice in the Swiss Alps used dogs to find lost travellers as early as the 17th century. Today, teams of rescue dogs operate throughout the world. They train with dummies first – then with live volunteers buried under the snow. Modern St Bernards are too heavy for this work; Border Collies and German Shepherds have taken their place.

Blitz dogs

During World War II, dogs proved better than people at searching bomb sites for the injured and dead. Beauty the Wire-haired Terrier was one canine heroine of the London Blitz. She alone found 63 casualties, and was awarded a medal for her war work.

Gundogs

The Brittany Spaniel (4) is still a working breed, but the Labrador (2), first bred as a retriever, is now popular as a an assistance dog and pet.

The Irish Setter (3) has striking good looks, which make it a popular pet. It is now rarely seen as a gundog. The Bracco Italiano (1), an eager worker, is also winning popularity in the show ring.

A keen sense of smell, boundless energy and a kind nature make gundogs ideal law enforcement recruits. To them, sniffing out drugs or explosives is a marvellous game – but their skill saves countless lives. One American Customs service dog, a Golden Retriever, found $60 million worth of smuggled drugs in one year.

On camera

Where humans cannot go, a search dog can – and now it can provide a running report to its handler, thanks to a mini video camera and microphone mounted on its head. Police and rescue workers use camera-carrying dogs to transmit scenes from earthquakes and terrorist attacks.

Sniffer dogs even help in wildlife conservation. Labradors are replacing radio collars for tracking wild animals in the USA. In Britain, Pointers help scientists to find and protect the nests of rare black grouse.

To the point

The thrill of the scent locks a Pointer into this rigid position. Even a very young puppy shows this strong drive, pointing at bumblebees in the absence of serious business.

23

Herding dogs

Looking after livestock may seem a far cry from hunting them, but it is the wolf's hunting instinct that enables farm dogs to herd sheep and cattle. Shepherd and dog work together like members of a wolf pack – the dog directs the flock's movements, just as his wild ancestors drove their prey towards their pack mates. Over time, herdsmen bred specialist sheep and cattle dogs which were tough, clever and had a built-in drive to work. Today, many excel at obedience work. But without plenty of physical and mental exercise, working dogs may become bored and destructive.

Hairy hypnotist
The Border Collie is the all-time sheep specialist. Developed to work free-ranging flocks in the wilds of Scotland, the Borders and Wales, the breed now aids sheep farmers worldwide. Noted for the 'strong eye', which it uses to control sheep with an almost hypnotic glare, the Border Collie is highly intelligent and is a top obedience breed.

Sheepdogs played a big part in the taming of the Wild West. When the US sheep industry took off in the 1840s (and 'range wars' broke out between cattle men and shepherds competing for good grazing land), collies were essential for moving flocks several thousand strong. Collies still fulfill this important job all over the world.

▲ Heavy, weather-proof coats are a feature of many European herding breeds, such as this Polish Lowland Sheepdog.

▼ Less well-known today than the Rough Collie, the Smooth Collie is an ancient Scottish breed.

▼ Now rarely worked, the Pembroke Corgi was bred as a cattle dog. Low to the ground, it drove cows by nipping at their heels.

Dog star
Film heroine Lassie is probably the most famous and best-loved dog in the world. She made the Rough Collie a breed everyone knows.

◄ Developed in the 1800s from various collie types and the native wild Dingo, the Australian Cattle Dog is a tough working breed.

Herding dogs were bred in various shapes and sizes to do different jobs. Large, powerful dogs such as the Maremma protected flocks from wolves. Small Swedish Valhunds directed stubborn cattle by snapping at their heels, while tough Bearded Collies drove herds hundreds of kilometres to market. The Shetland Islands, famed for dwarf sheep and ponies, produced a mini-dog – the Shetland Sheepdog.

Noisy worker
The New Zealand Huntaway is unusual among sheepdogs in that it barks while it works. Driving the sheep from behind, it urges them on vocally.

Beware of the dog

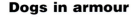

Just as wolves guard their home and family, the first dogs turned their keen senses, protective urge and fighting ability to guarding their human masters – a task performed to this day. At times, they also fought beside their owners in war. By 2000BC, the war dogs of Babylon struck fear into opposing armies.

Dogs in armour
In the Middle Ages, war dogs wore leather and chainmail armour to attack mounted knights. They were highly effective until the development of gunpowder meant their armour no longer gave them sufficient protection.

The heavy squad
Of these four flock-guarding breeds, only the Bouvier des Flandres and Komondor are likely to be found working in their original role today.

To the rescue
It's not just fierce dogs that protect their owners. Nottie, a gentle Golden Retriever, came to the rescue when his owner was attacked by a herd of cows. By racing to fetch help, he saved his owner's life – and wears his life-saver's medal with pride.

Wherever wolves roamed, or human enemies raided, farmers relied on dogs to protect their flocks and herds. Big, tough and intelligent, many of these flock-guarding breeds, such as the German Shepherd Dog, are still valued today as protective companions.

Bouvier des Flandres

Rottweiler

German Shepherd Dog

Komondor

Celtic colossus
In Roman times, the giant war dogs that accompanied Celtic tribes into battle were famous. Such fierce hounds were a fitting emblem for a warrior, as depicted on this Celtic shield.

Pictures of power
Roman householders relied on guard dogs to protect their property. Floor mosaics depicting these guardians weren't just decorative, but warned burglars to 'Beware of the dog'.

Seeing eyes
Guide dogs give blind people back their independence. The special harness, worn only when the dog is working, lets the owner feel when the dog reaches a step or slope in the path.

Hearing dogs
Hearing dogs for the deaf are trained to alert their owners to all sorts of important sounds, from everyday alarm clocks and doorbells to fire alarms, boiling kettles or crying babies.

Guides and helpers

Dogs have been trained to lead the blind for at least 2,000 years, but we have only recently come to appreciate just how much help a well-trained dog can give its owner. Today we have not only 'seeing eye' dogs for the blind, but 'hearing ear' dogs for the deaf and even assistance dogs for the disabled.

A helping paw
Assistance dogs help their disabled owners with a wide range of everyday tasks. They carry shopping, fetch named objects like cordless telephones, operate buttons for lifts and pedestrian crossings and even load and unload the washing machine.

Opening doors
People on crutches and in wheelchairs can't open doors very easily, so a canine helper comes in handy. But a support dog also opens the door to an independent life for a disabled owner.

Mountain rescue dogs sniff out lost hikers and avalanche victims where human searchers are helpless. With its keen sense of smell, and two years' careful training, one dog can do the work of ten men on such missions. Search and rescue dogs have saved many lives, but off-duty, they are just normal family pets.

Acting as a handicapped person's eyes, ears or as a helping hand takes a special kind of dog. Golden Retrievers and Labradors are particularly well suited to 'the caring professions', but other breeds also serve. Many training organisations breed their own puppies for the job. Others welcome suitable pups donated by breeders or even pick likely-looking recruits from animal rescue shelters. Trainees which don't make the grade as workers are found pet homes.

Hospital helpers
Specially trained dogs are welcome visitors in many old people's homes and hospitals. They can sense who needs company or comfort, and sometimes patients who have withdrawn from human contact respond better to a dog's silent sympathy.

Puppy walkers
Puppies bred to be guides and helpers are fostered for their first year by volunteer 'puppy walkers' – people who give them basic schooling. This prepares them for specialist training.

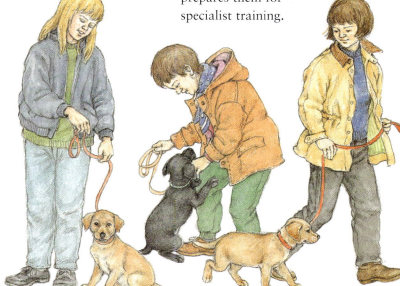

The lap of luxury

Dogs do not have to be workers to be valued. From ancient times, miniature dogs of no practical use were treasured as luxury items by the rich. Their only 'work' was to amuse and love their owners. Needing little space and exercise, mini-dogs are still popular today.

The Papillon (1), Toy Poodle (2) and Cavalier King Charles Spaniel (4) descend from European sporting breeds. The Pug (3) and Shih Tzu (5) are Orientals, and the tiny Chihuahua (6) is an American creation.

Friends at court
Over the ages, lapdogs have been despised as useless by some and adored as comforters by others. The Middle Ages saw mini-breeds such as the Papillon, Volpino and King Charles Spaniel established as royal favourites in Europe.

Richard Burton and Elizabeth Taylor are just two of the many film stars who appreciated the fashion for decorative little dogs as pets.

In the East, decorative miniature dogs adorned imperial courts and Buddhist monasteries. China produced short-faced *ha-pa* ('under-the-table') dogs, ancestors of our Pugs, and the 'lion dog' – the Pekingese – bred in the image of the Buddhist symbol of the lion.

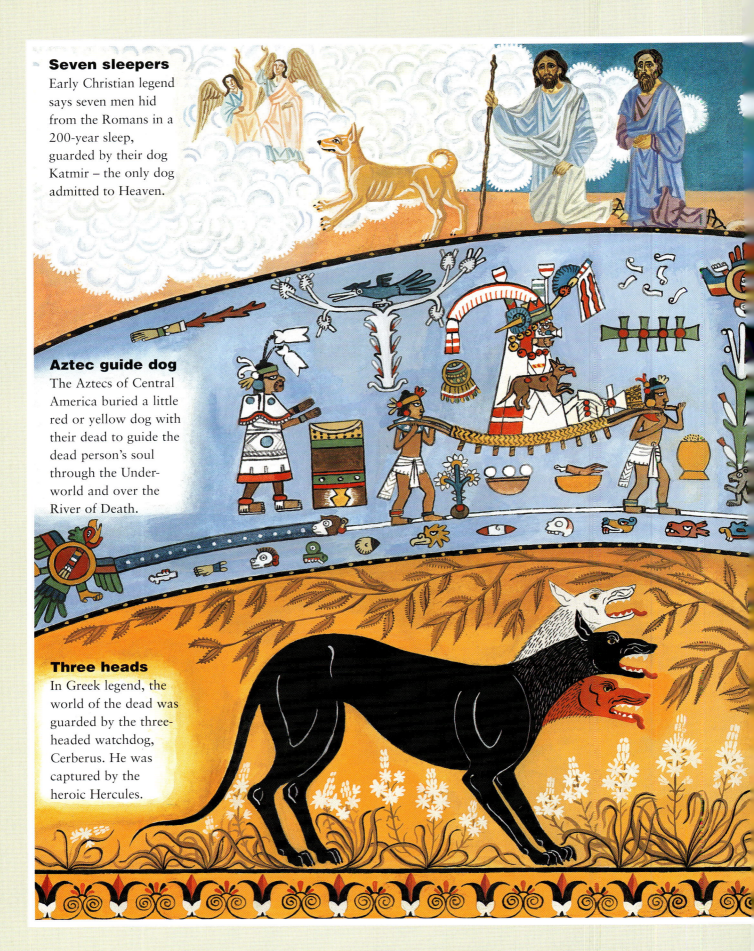

Seven sleepers
Early Christian legend says seven men hid from the Romans in a 200-year sleep, guarded by their dog Katmir – the only dog admitted to Heaven.

Aztec guide dog
The Aztecs of Central America buried a little red or yellow dog with their dead to guide the dead person's soul through the Underworld and over the River of Death.

Three heads
In Greek legend, the world of the dead was guarded by the three-headed watchdog, Cerberus. He was captured by the heroic Hercules.

DOG MYTHOLOGY

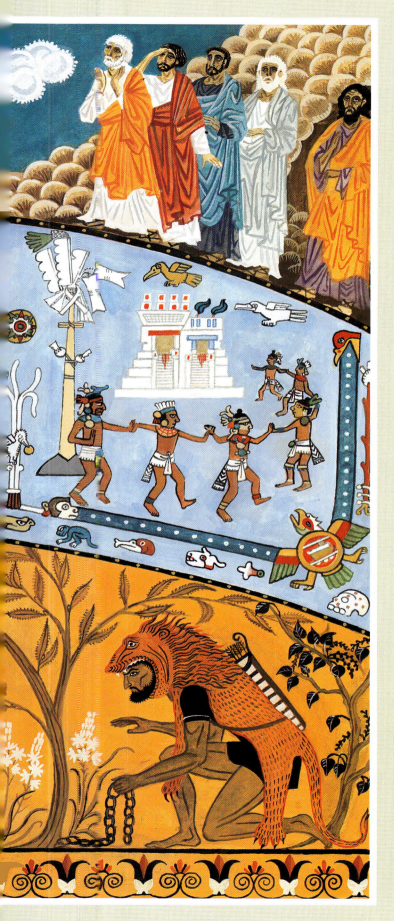

The wolf has always lurked on the dark side of mythology, and the legend of the werewolf remains familiar today. The dog's role is less simple. Some religions regarded it as unclean and ungodly, perhaps because of its scavenging habits. But many others honoured it as a trusted guardian. From Ancient Egypt, where the jackal-headed god Anubis led the souls of the dead to judgement, to medieval Mexico, where the Chihuahua guided its master's soul across the River of Death, the dog watched over the gateway leading from our world to the next.

When Buddhism spread to China and Japan, the lion (Buddha's symbol) posed a problem to artists unfamiliar with lions. The result was the creation of the Lion Dog, or Fo Dog – part dragon, part Pekingese. Fo Dog statues adorn temples throughout the East. Many wear the tasselled collar and bells traditionally worn by Pekingese at the Chinese royal court.

33

In Ancient Egypt, Sirius the Dog Star was believed to be the watchdog of the River Nile. The seasonal appearance of Sirius, the brightest star in the sky, announced the coming of the flood season, which gave people time to move to high ground.

Magical dogs

Dogs accompany their masters in legend as in life, playing their role as faithful guardians. Even Noah's Ark relied on the dog, which plugged a leak with its nose – and this is why, so legend goes, dogs still have a cold, damp nose.

Associated in Egyptian mythology with Sirius the Dog Star is the fertility goddess Isis. The rising of Sirius coincided with the flooding of the Nile – and these flood waters were said to be the tears of Isis weeping for her slain brother Osiris, bringing fertility to the Nile plains.

Patience rewarded
In Greek legend, the faithful dog Argos waited 20 years for his master Ulysses to return from the Trojan War. When at last the wanderer returned, only Argos recognised him. He licked his master's hand, and died in contentment soon after.

Keeping faith
Indian king Yudhishthira refused to enter Heaven without his faithful dog – an 'unclean' animal. His loyalty was rewarded, for the dog was actually the god Indra in disguise.

Throughout European mythology, magical packs of hounds stream across the night sky. Sometimes they hunt the Moon, sometimes the souls of men. The leader of the hunt may be a pagan deity, from Greek Artemis to Norse Odin, or a hero such as King Arthur. In Cornish folklore he is wicked Squire Dando, who went hunting on the Sabbath and now must hunt for ever.

Arthur's hound
Welsh legend says that Britain's legendary King Arthur owned the mighty hound Cavall, who helped him capture the magical boar Twrch Trwyth.

Guardian ghost
At Rose Hill in Maryland, USA, a sinister blue ghost dog is said to guard the buried gold of his master, who was murdered by thieves in the 1860s.

When the fairies ride at night, you may hear their white, red-eared hounds baying as they race across the sky – though the less romantic may hear only the hound-like cry of wild geese. The fairy hounds are also the Hounds of Hell, hunting mortal souls.

Choosing a dog

Making the choice between male or female, pedigree or mongrel, puppy or adult is up to you. All can make fine pets. Mongrels are not necessarily healthier, but if you decide on a pedigree, read up on any inherited disorders in the breed, and make sure the breeder has carried out any necessary health tests. Puppies are endearing but hard work; adults may arrive ready-trained, but may equally have some well-established bad habits. Your new friend may be with you for the next ten to twenty years, so choose carefully.

Good home needed
Adopting a dog from a rescue kennels can be extremely rewarding. It can also be very hard. Some rescue dogs have had a bad start in life and need experienced new owners to re-educate them. Others have already been loved and trained as delightful companions. A good rescue home will offer guidance and will try to match dogs to suitable owners.

Be careful where you obtain your new friend – look for a caring breeder or a rescue kennels that works hard at matching dogs to new owners. Expect breeders to give you a good grilling to make sure you are a suitable owner: it is a bad sign if they don't care where their puppies end up. And don't be afraid to ask questions yourself.

Good homes needed for pups

Golden Retriever puppies, to approved homes only. Home-reared with children. Wormed, registered and insured. Parents hip-scored and eye-tested clear. After-sales service.
Tel: 557 9121

DOGS FOR SALE

Yorkie, Poodle and German Shepherd puppies and adults. Other breeds often available.
Tel: 269 2255

Cute Corgi cross pups, 15 weeks old.
Tel: 262 9071

Choose carefully
Read between the lines in advertisements. 'Puppy farmers' offer quantity rather than quality. Their puppies are often badly cared for and may never achieve good full health. Nothing can replace the good start supplied by a caring breeder.

Golden Retriever

Family friends
If you're a first-time dog owner, it's sensible to pick a breed that's easy to live with. Golden Retrievers have a well-earned reputation as reliable family dogs, but do need plenty of exercise and grooming. The Norfolk Terrier is a bundle of fun in smaller form with typical terrier bounce.

Norfolk Terrier

Be sure
Before you buy that appealing pup, make sure you can cope with its adult needs. If you fancy a bouncy Boxer, consider whether you can handle that bumptious energy. If you fall for an Old English Sheepdog, will you enjoy all that grooming? The wrong choice may mean misery for both of you.

Old English Sheepdog

Look for a dog that's healthy in mind and body. Some breeds are less outgoing than others, but it's safest to pick a puppy that likes the look of you. Over-bold, bossy pups and scaredy-cats are going to be hard work, so avoid these two and go for the happy, responsive youngster in the middle. Take extra care when choosing an adult dog.

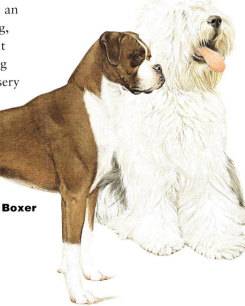
Boxer

Canine care

 Your dog's practical needs are for food, water, grooming, exercise and somewhere to sleep. Pet shops stock a bewildering variety of kit, but you don't need all of it. Either fresh or manufactured food is suitable, but red meat alone does not contain all the minerals and vitamins a dog needs. Fresh water is a must, so keep that water-bowl full.

Plain or fancy
Luxury collars, beds and bowls interest owners more than dogs. A dog will be just as happy with much more basic equipment – so long as the bowl has food in it!

Bedtime

A comfy, draught-proof and easily cleaned bed is essential. Avoid beds which can be chewed into sharp edges. Puppies may be best with a cardboard box, easily replaced when soiled or chewed. All bedding needs regular flea treatment.

Walkies

Your dog needs a collar with address tag and lead. A buckled leather collar is most comfortable. Choke chains are best avoided: it is all too easy to hurt the dog with these. Dogs which pull may be better with a head collar, which gives you more control. An extending lead can be useful if you can't yet trust your dog off-leash.

Wild dogs attend to their own fur, but most pet dogs need help. For shortcoats, a brisk weekly brush keeps skin healthy and massages muscles; most longcoats need daily care. Heavy-coated dogs such as the Old English Sheepdog suffer discomfort after a few days without grooming and a few months' neglect can mean a trip to the vet. Grooming is a matter of healthcare, but it is also a way of showing affection and a chance to remind a bossy dog who's in charge.

Brushing
A natural bristle brush suits most types of coat. Work through the whole coat gently, first against the direction of the hair and then the right way.

Polishing off
For dogs with short to medium coats, finish off by smoothing the fur over with a rubber brush or even a silk cloth to give it a real shine.

Comb with care
Longer hair needs combing through to remove tangles, but be careful not to pull the hair. A wide-toothed metal comb is safest.

Dinner time
Puppies need several small meals a day, adult dogs either one large meal or two smaller ones morning and evening. Most dogs will eat more food than is good for them, so keep an eye on your dog's figure.

Playtime
Toys are fun – and are also good training aids. But some toys on sale are dangerous. Beware cheap toys which can be chewed and swallowed, and small balls which can stick in a dog's throat and choke it.

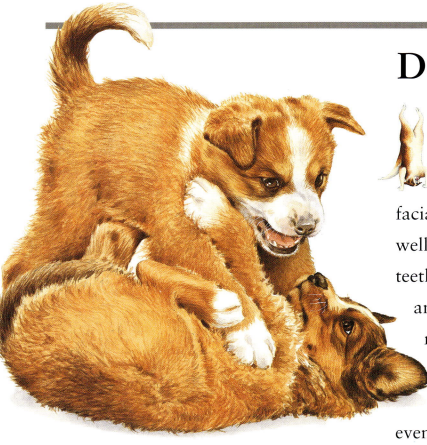

Dog language

Dogs try very hard to understand us, and we can help by trying to understand their sign language of facial expression and body posture, as well as voice. A friendly tail-wag or a teeth-baring snarl are easily understood, and most owners soon learn to recognise other gestures and expressions. You can tell a lot from a dog's face, and some dogs even learn to copy the human smile, drawing back their lips and showing their teeth just like us.

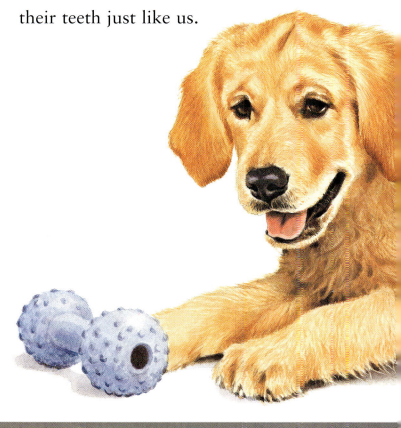

Other animals
Dogs don't speak 'cat' or any other animal language. When a puppy greets a kitten with a welcoming bounce, the kitten may well think it's being attacked. You will need to introduce your dog to other pets carefully. It takes time and patience to build up friendship between different species.

Who's boss?
Dogs express social status by position: the dominant dog 'stands tall', while the submissive underdog grovels. The business of who is top dog and who is underdog is often important in canine relationships and is established at an early stage while dogs are still puppies. A dog also needs to know in its relationship with its owner whether the dog or the human is 'pack leader'. Letting the dog be boss doesn't work very well. Knowing that somebody else is in charge makes a dog feel more secure and therefore easier to train.

Let's play

A classic example of the dog's body language, and one of a dog's most charming gestures, is the invitation to play. The dog lowers its front end, while holding its hindquarters and tail high in a posture known as the play-bow. The face is relaxed, with an open mouth that looks as if it is laughing. The message is clear: 'Come on, let's play!'

Keep clear!

Dogs announce their intention to attack with clear signals. The aggressive dog draws itself up to its full height with ears and tail high, bared teeth and a threatening stare. Even more dangerous is the nervous dog driven to attack by fear: the corners of the mouth are drawn back, the ears flattened and the tail held low. Always respect a threat display and keep well clear.

Saying Hello
When you approach a strange dog, the fact that you are taller can look like a threat. Crouch down and offer a hand from a safe distance so the dog can choose to come and investigate. Never approach a dog without asking its owner first.

Messages received by the nose play a large part in communication between dogs. When two dogs meet, they smell each other first, just as we shake hands or say 'Hello'. Dogs greet us in the same way, and learn a lot about us from our scent.

The well-trained dog

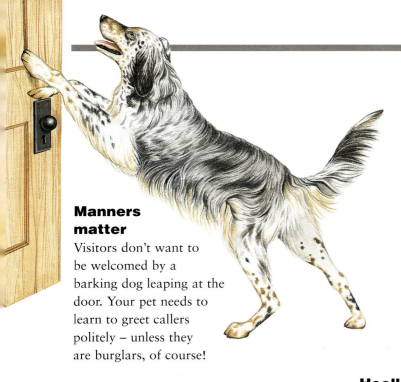

Dogs which have been taught how to fit in with our lives are happier as well as nicer to live with. Most dogs are keen to learn, but we sometimes make it hard for them. Training takes time, patience and awareness of how dogs see the world. Remember, they don't speak English!

Manners matter
Visitors don't want to be welcomed by a barking dog leaping at the door. Your pet needs to learn to greet callers politely – unless they are burglars, of course!

Heel!
Walking a dog that pulls on the lead is no fun for either of you. Puppies learn good manners easily, but you may need help with an older dog which has learned bad habits.

Fetch!
A well-trained dog is a pleasure to live with, and gets pleasure from pleasing you. Gundogs just love to retrieve, and can make themselves really useful fetching and carrying for you.

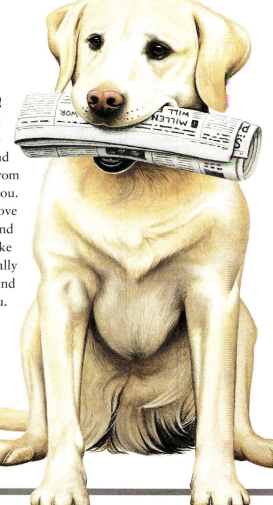

Digger dogs
Don't leave your new puppy to amuse himself alone in the garden, but stay with him to teach him the rules. Dogs don't know about lawns and roses, but they do know it's fun to dig – unless you teach them otherwise.

Training classes, where you can learn to train your dog, are offered in most areas. Some teach basic good behaviour, others teach competitive obedience, agility or how to show a dog. A good class is also a social club for your dog, where it can meet friends – and learn not to be distracted by them. It is also a great social club for dog-loving humans!

Ground rules
Military-style obedience isn't necessary in a pet, but sensible behaviour is. Learning to walk on a slack lead, sit, come when called, and stay will ensure your dog doesn't get into trouble.

High jinks
Many dogs enjoy agility training, learning to complete an obstacle course with jumps and tunnels. It's great fun as well as healthy exercise – but not for puppies, who might strain themselves.

Sit!
This is one of the most useful commands. A dog which sits when told is always under control. You can take him anywhere and rely on his behaviour being a credit to you.

Best in show
Show dogs have to learn how to behave in the show ring – walking nicely, letting the judge examine them, and so on. They also need to learn that showing is fun: a nervous or unhappy dog won't look good enough to impress the judges.

Breeds of dog

Worldwide, more than 400 breeds of dog are recognised. Many you may never see, either because they are extremely rare or because they are found only in their own country. Some breeds, such as the Old English White Terrier and the Welsh Hillman Herder, have become extinct in recent years.

Obviously, we can't fit 400 dogs on this page. What we can show is a sample of the large and the small, the swift and the slow, the clever, the strong the handsome and the hardworking. Breeds have been assigned to one of three groups, made up of sporting dogs, working dogs and companions.

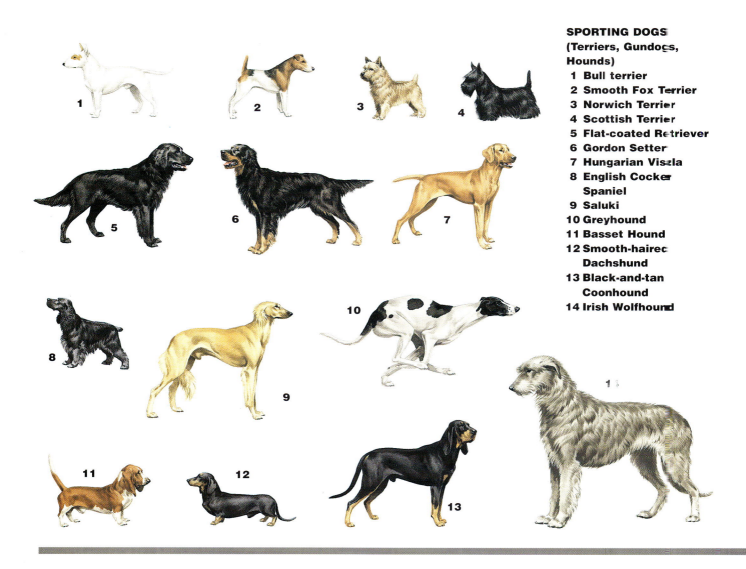

SPORTING DOGS
(Terriers, Gundogs, Hounds)
1. Bull terrier
2. Smooth Fox Terrier
3. Norwich Terrier
4. Scottish Terrier
5. Flat-coated Retriever
6. Gordon Setter
7. Hungarian Vizsla
8. English Cocker Spaniel
9. Saluki
10. Greyhound
11. Basset Hound
12. Smooth-haired Dachshund
13. Black-and-tan Coonhound
14. Irish Wolfhound

WORKING DOGS
(Guards, Haulers, Herders)
15 Neapolitan Mastiff
16 Rottweiler
17 Bullmastiff
18 Great Dane
19 Siberian Husky
20 Samoyed
21 Alaskan Malamute
22 Japanese Akita
23 Pembroke Welsh Corgi
24 Shetland Sheepdog
25 Belgian Shepherd Dog
   (Groenendael)
26 Briard
27 Pyrenean Mountain
   Dog

COMPANIONS
(including Toy dogs)
28 Dalmatian
29 Bulldog
30 Newfoundland
31 St Bernard
32 Elkhound
33 Lhasa Apso
34 Tibetan Spaniel
35 Cavalier King
   Charles Spaniel
36 Bichon Frise
37 Miniature Poodle
38 Lowchen
39 Maltese

45

CAT FAMILY

From mighty lions to humble moggies, cats form an instantly recognizable family. They may come in different sizes and colours, but all cats share the same graceful shape. Highly successful hunters, all species of cat are carnivores – they all eat meat.

▼ The shy marbled cat – a mini clouded leopard – is an endangered species. It is only slightly larger than most domestic (pet) cats.

◄ Despite its name, southern Asia's most common wild cat, the leopard cat, doesn't really look like its big cousin. It has rows of spots instead of the leopard's rosette patterns.

◀ A forest dweller that spends much of its life in the trees, the beautiful clouded leopard is smaller than a leopard. For its size, this cat has the biggest teeth of all the felines: it's nicknamed 'the modern sabre-tooth'!

▲ Little is known about the flat-headed cat, except that it hunts fish and frogs along forest riverbanks. Its long body, short legs and flattened head make it look a bit like a domestic cat that's been squashed!

The cat family can be divided into three groups. The smallest group (*Acinonyx*) contains only one species, the cheetah. The dog-like cheetah differs from other cats so much that it is classed on its own: it is the only cat to usually outsprint its prey rather than stalk it. The two main cat groups are the big cats (*Panthera*), such as lions and tigers, and the little cats (*Felis*). Apart from size, the main distinction is that big cats roar, and little cats purr. Some medium-sized cats, such as the clouded leopard, don't quite fit with the big or little cats. Zoologists are still arguing about how to class these cats.

Different voice-boxes explain why big cats roar and little cats purr. Big cats have an elastic 'sounding board' in the throat which amplifies their roar to give a booming effect.

Little cats can purr for hours on end. As the cat breathes in and out, air passes over an extra, 'false' pair of vocal cords. This makes a rumbling sound rather like a human snore!

Evolution of the cat

The story of cats begins some sixty million years ago, with a small, weasel-like carnivore called *Miacis*. This was probably the ancestor of all modern carnivores, including dogs and bears as well as cats. The first recognizably cat-like animal, *Dinictis*, evolved ten million years later. Its modern descendants include all the cats.

Distant cousins
Civets, genets and mongooses (the *Viverridae* family) are also descended from *Dinictis*. So this genet is a distant cousin of the cat tribe – a closer relation than the bear or the dog.

genet

From little *Miacis* and medium-sized *Dinictis* sprang all cats, great and small. The modern cat family numbers 36 wild species.

Alongside the domestic cat (*Felis catus*), the other little cats include: the African wildcat, black-footed cat, bobcat, cougar, fishing cat, jungle cat, lynx, manul, margay, ocelot, sand cat and serval. The tiger, lion, leopard and jaguar make up the big cats.

The cheetah isn't classed with the big cats or the little cats. It developed separately and became the world's fastest land animal. Its top speed is a record-breaking 96km/h.

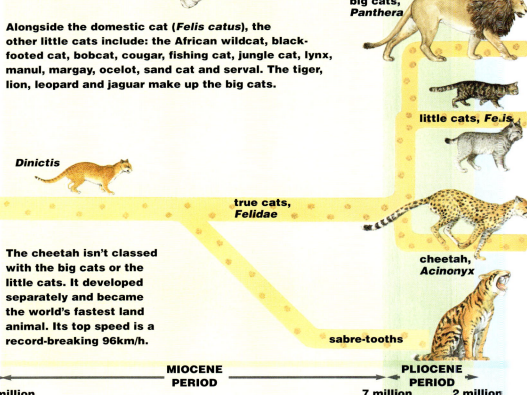

big cats, *Panthera*
little cats, *Felis*
true cats, *Felidae*
cheetah, *Acinonyx*
sabre-tooths
Dinictis
Miacis

OLIGOCENE PERIOD — MIOCENE PERIOD — PLIOCENE PERIOD

35 million years ago | 25 million years ago | 7 million years ago | 2 million years ago

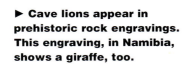

▶ Cave lions appear in prehistoric rock engravings. This engraving, in Namibia, shows a giraffe, too.

The early cat family split into two branches: sabre-tooths and true cats. Sabre-tooths were big and powerful, but relatively small-brained. They lived on Earth for almost thirty-four million years. The sabre-tooths died out around twelve thousand years ago and left no modern descendants. The early true cats also included large animals such as the cave lion. Little cats evolved about twelve million years ago. As cats spread across the world, through Asia, Africa, Europe and the Americas, a variety of species developed. The wildcat, ancestor of our pets, first appeared over one-and-a-half million years ago.

Fang monster
Sabre-tooths, such as *Smilodon*, are so called because they had extremely long canine teeth. When they hunted mammoths and other large beasts, they used their canines like sabres (swords) to stab their prey.

Smilodon

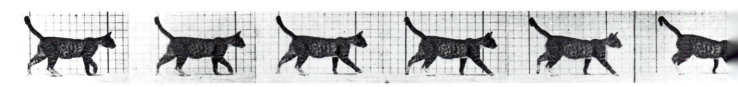

The elastic skeleton

A cat's body is so flexible it seems almost boneless. It can twist and turn at incredible angles, stretch out for a streamlined pounce, or squeeze through the tiniest gap.

Bones are solid objects which can't really be elastic, so how does the cat manage this? The answer lies in the design of its skeleton. Like ours, the cat's backbone is made up of a chain of small bones called vertebrae. But the cat's vertebrae are much more loosely connected than ours, making the spine much bendier. In addition, the cat's forelegs can move much more freely from the shoulder than our arms. Covered by superbly supple muscles and a loose skin, the cat's body is designed for gymnastics!

Cat work-out

Artists have long been fascinated by the cat's suppleness. In this book, you'll see that there are as many ways of painting a cat as there are cats! These black-and-white studies come from a book of picture stories about cats by a French artist at the turn of the century. They celebrate the flowing curves into which cats twist their elastic bodies – whether they are awake or asleep.

◀ **'Paresse' from *Des Chats*, by Théophile Steinlen**

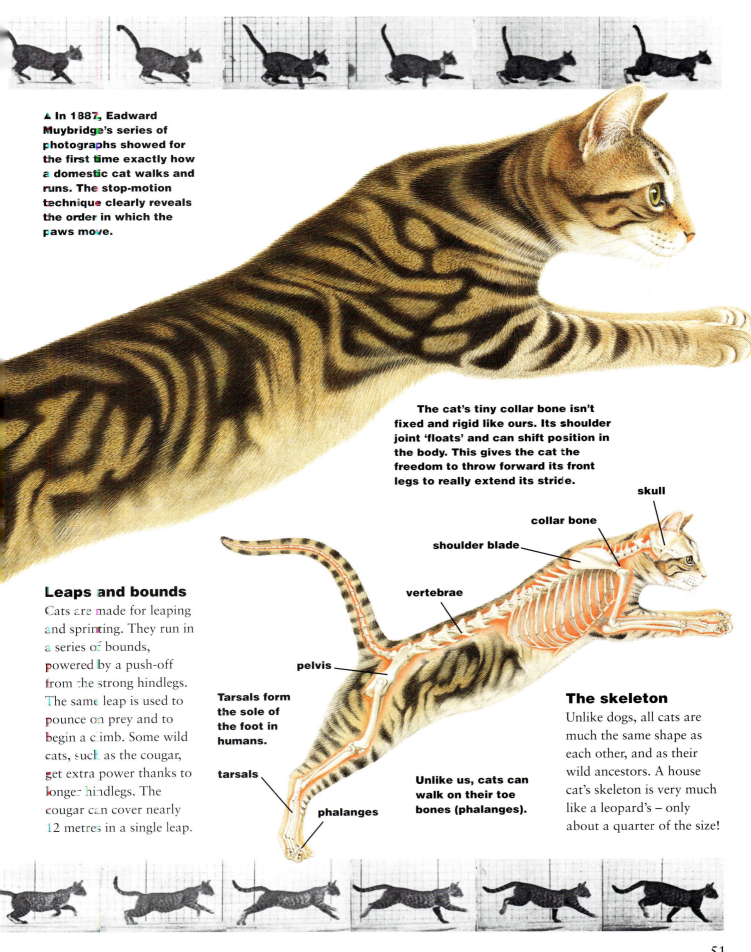

▲ In 1887, Eadward Muybridge's series of photographs showed for the first time exactly how a domestic cat walks and runs. The stop-motion technique clearly reveals the order in which the paws move.

The cat's tiny collar bone isn't fixed and rigid like ours. Its shoulder joint 'floats' and can shift position in the body. This gives the cat the freedom to throw forward its front legs to really extend its stride.

Leaps and bounds

Cats are made for leaping and sprinting. They run in a series of bounds, powered by a push-off from the strong hindlegs. The same leap is used to pounce on prey and to begin a climb. Some wild cats, such as the cougar, get extra power thanks to longer hindlegs. The cougar can cover nearly 12 metres in a single leap.

Tarsals form the sole of the foot in humans.

Unlike us, cats can walk on their toe bones (phalanges).

The skeleton

Unlike dogs, all cats are much the same shape as each other, and as their wild ancestors. A house cat's skeleton is very much like a leopard's – only about a quarter of the size!

51

Balancing tricks

Cats are never clumsy. A wonderful sense of balance allows them to climb to dangerous heights or walk along the narrowest ledge. Even when cats do fall, they're famous for always landing on their feet – they have been known to survive a fall of 32 storeys, without fatal injury.

The acrobat
Tightrope-walking the top of a narrow fence is easy for the cat, setting each paw exactly in front of the other. The cat can even turn round halfway without falling. To do this, it balances on its hindlegs and pushes its forelegs as far back as possible, then shifts its weight to them before swinging its hindquarters round. Cats learn this skill as kittens, but practice makes perfect!

On your feet!
Flying cats and water form graceful curves in this unusual portrait of artist Salvador Dali. It took the photographer's four assistants and three good-natured cats 26 attempts to achieve the desired result!

▲ *Dali Atomicus*, by Philippe Halsman

Climbing
The cat begins its climb with a leap at the fence, then grabs hold with its claws. Having got a grip, it pulls itself up with its powerful forelegs. Coming down is harder: most cats prefer to jump than to ease down backwards.

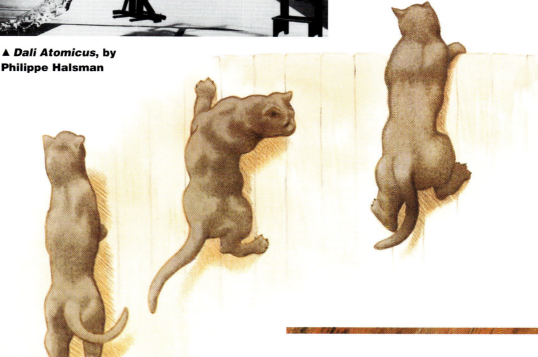

A safe landing

The cat uses its eyes and ears to ensure that it will always fall on its feet. In mid-air (1), the eyes and a finely-tuned balance organ in the ears send messages to the brain, identifying the direction of gravity's pull. Now the cat can pinpoint the exact position of its head in relation to the ground. The cat rights its head first (2), then twists its body into line until its feet point downwards (3). The outstretched tail helps it to balance as it lands feet first (4).

High and mighty

Climbing is a skill common to all cats, though some species use it more than others. The champion climber is the South American margay. This little cat spends most of its life in the trees where it hunts, nests and rears its kittens high among the branches.

Tree-climbing gives cats a high-rise hunting-ground. So many birds and small animals feed in the branches that the treetop world is like a cats' supermarket! Trees also provide safe hiding-places from a cat's enemies, look-out posts for spotting prey, and shelter from the sun's heat. Most little cat species are at home in the trees, but even lions are known to make use of this higher level.

Teeth and claws

Head of a hunter
A look at the cat's skull shows us the teeth of a meat-eater. They are designed to bite, tear and chop, but not to chew. Cats swallow their food without chewing it up. Instead, the stomach breaks down the food with digestive juices.

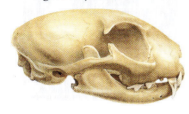

The killing bite
Wild cats must kill in order to live, and a stabbing blow from their long canine teeth to the back of the victim's neck brings a quick death. Domestic cats can kill in just the same way as this leopard, though in both cases youngsters have to learn how to deliver the killing bite. Many pet cats never master it.

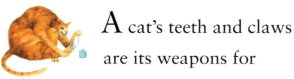

A cat's teeth and claws are its weapons for fighting and its tools for hunting. Long canine teeth – the cat family's trademark – can hold and kill prey, and tear meat. The back teeth serve as cutlery, to cut food into manageable pieces. The front teeth, the incisors, are small, for nibbling. Sharp claws help to give the cat a good grip on its prey. They are also one of the reasons why cats can climb so well: the cat uses them as grappling hooks to hang on as it works its way upwards.

Claws and teeth are deadly weapons – so cats control their use. Most cat fights involve more screeching and glaring than actual bites and scratches.

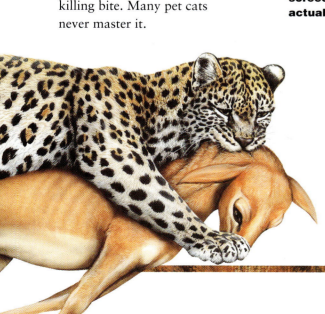

Claws

Claws are too important to risk blunting them, so they are sheathed (1) when not in use. Small ligaments (bands of elastic tissue) attached to the toe bones hold the claws inside the paw. Larger ligaments pull back to let the claws flash out (2) when needed.

The cat's armoury consists of 30 teeth (except for two wild species, the lynx and Pallas's cat, with 28 teeth each) and 18 claws – four on each hind paw and five on each forepaw with the fifth, the dew claw, tucked up the back of each foreleg.

All cat species, except the dog-like cheetah, can sheathe (cover) their claws to protect the points. The fishing cat, though, doesn't have quite the full equipment. Its claws are too big for their sheaths, and don't tuck away completely.

Claw manicure

Claws grow throughout life, like our nails. When we see a cat scrape its claws down a tree (or a chair!), we often say it is sharpening its claws. It is actually stripping them – scratching off the worn outer coat of its claws to reveal new, sharp tips.

55

The fur coat

More than just a coat, the cat's fur is a complete outfit! It serves, like our clothes, to keep out the cold – and excess heat. It is protective gear to save the skin from scratches and camouflage gear, the colour or pattern helping to hide the cat from its prey – or from enemies. Finally, the coat is a notice-board which bears scent messages for other cats to read. It also signals a threat when it is fluffed out in fear or anger, making the cat look bigger and fiercer.

Thick fur protects against the cold, especially when the cat fluffs up its coat. A layer of warm air gets trapped under the fur, next to the skin. This makes an efficient 'thermal vest'. However, of course a pet cat can always come inside when it's had enough of the great outdoors!

Layers of hairs

Wild cats, and most domestic ones, wear a two-layered coat. The colourful and protective top coat consists of long, strong guard hairs.

Next to the skin lies the undercoat of short, fluffy fur, like a warm vest. This is made up of down hairs, which are very short and soft, and awn hairs, slightly longer and coarser.

○ guard hair
● awn hair
○ down hair

Persian

Shorthair

Fur fashions

Pedigrees are bred for special kinds of coat. Shorthairs (1) have the same three-layered coat as their wild ancestors. Persians (2) have extremely long fur, with no awn hairs. The Somali (3) is an example of a longhair with a medium-length fluffy coat (sometimes called a semi-longhair). Two unusual coat types belong to the American Wirehair (4) which has short, wavy and wiry fur, and the Cornish Rex (5) whose coat is short, curly and without guard hairs. Strangest of all is the virtually hairless Sphynx (6), which doesn't even have whiskers.

Sandshoes

Going barefoot on scorching sand is very uncomfortable – and it's no different with bare paws. The sand cat lives in the deserts of Africa and Asia and solves the problem by wearing furry slippers! Long tufts of fur protect its pads from the burning sand.

We don't wear winter coats in summer, and neither do cats. They adapt to the seasons by moulting twice a year – shedding the old coat to grow a new one, thicker in winter and lighter in summer. Our domestic cats have lost some of this moulting pattern. Most shed a few hairs all year round.

Cats' eyes

Sight is very important to cats. Their eyes are hunters' eyes – large, and designed for spotting prey. They are particularly alert to sudden movements.

Lynx-eyed
The keen-eyed lynx can spot a grouse from 300 metres away – the length of three football pitches. Not surprisingly, in ancient times this cat was a symbol of acute sight, and we still describe observant people as 'lynx-eyed'. Actually, most members of the cat family have equally good vision.

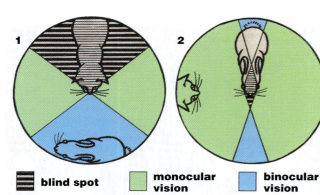

blind spot | monocular vision | binocular vision

For sharp focus, an object needs to be seen by both eyes at once. This is binocular ('two-eyed') vision. Focusing with only one eye (monocular vision) picks out movement but not distance. Cats (1) have a very wide binocular area of vision, for sharp focus on their prey. In contrast rabbits (2) have a much wider field of monocular vision – making it harder for hunters to creep up on them unseen.

Cats' vision differs from ours in several ways. They can see in light at least six times dimmer than we can, though even cats can't see in pitch darkness. They can't make out fine detail and small objects as well as we do, but they don't need to. Their colour vision isn't as good, either, but they aren't colour-blind, as was once thought.

58

Eye-opener

At night, the pupils of a cat's eye open wide to let in maximum light (top). By day, they can avoid dazzle by narrowing to slits (bottom). Human eyes also adapt to light and dark, but not enough to cope with the near-darkness in which cats can see.

Night vision is aided by a 'mirror' (tapetum) at the back of the eye, which reflects what light there is.

An eye-shield

Extra protection for the cat's eyes comes from the third eyelid, known as the haw, or nictitating membrane. This is tucked away in the inner corner of each eye, moving across the eye occasionally to spread moisture over the surface. Most of the time it stays out of sight.

A cat whose third eyelids are permanently on display is showing signs of illness, and needs to visit the vet.

Eye colours

Domestic cats' eyes show an incredible colour range. Pedigrees must have the approved eye colour for their breed – blue for Siamese (1), and green for Chinchillas (3). Orange and yellow shades range from the Blue Persian's deep copper (2) to the Black Shorthair's gold (4). The Tabby Maine Coon (6) has hazel eyes and the Odd-Eyed White Persian (5) has one blue eye and one orange!

Cats' eyes don't change just to cope with different lighting conditions, but also to react to different situations. A cat threatening an enemy narrows its pupils more tightly to focus on the foe, but a threatened cat opens its eyes wide in a black-eyed stare. In both cases, the eyes are displaying a warning signal as clear as any words!

59

Large, mobile ears can turn towards a sound to pinpoint its source. The cat's ears can even pick up high-pitched sounds (such as a mouse's squeak) that humans cannot hear.

The cat's sense of smell is 30 times better than that of a human.

Taste matters less to cats than to us. As carnivores, cats have taste buds that identify meaty and fatty tastes. We humans have 18 times as many taste buds and we can therefore identify more types of taste than cats can.

Extra senses
Our simple world of five senses would seem boring to a cat. Whatever the claims for their 'sixth sense' special powers, they definitely have one extra sense! A special organ in the roof of the mouth, the Jacobsen's organ, can 'taste' scent particles in the air.

Whiskers are high-powered organs of touch. They can even detect air movements.

More senses

A hunter needs good hearing as well as good eyesight, and a cat's ears are designed for the job. The cat has an excellent sense of smell, too, though it doesn't rely on this to hunt. It uses its nose mainly to investigate food, and to 'read' the smell messages produced by other cats. The cat doesn't need much sense of taste, but its sense of touch is highly developed, with sensitive whiskers (on its wrists as well as its face) acting as feelers.

Cat mapping
Cats also have a special direction-finding sense. Far from home, the cat's built-in 'compass' allows it to map out the route back. Scientists are still investigating how this works. In April 1997, Sooty the cat hit the news. She had trekked 160 kilometres to return to her old home after her owners moved house. Sooty was sedated for the original car journey from Swansea, Wales, to Bath, England, but somehow still managed to find her way back to Wales. Sooty's incredible journey took six months!

Whisker work
As the cat pounces, its whiskers point forward to 'read' the shape, size and movements of its target.

Big ears
Its outsize ears tell us that the serval, an African wild cat, depends on its hearing to find prey. The least rustle in the grass allows it to pinpoint the location of a hidden mouse or rat – and pounce! Those sensitive ears can even pick up the sound of a mole rat tunnelling underground, so the serval knows just where to dig for dinner.

Cats' whiskers are highly sensitive feelers. With whiskers leading the way, the cat can detect the exact position, shape and size of everything it approaches – even in the dark. This helps it to pounce accurately on prey, and to know instantly whether a gap is wide enough to slip through. It also explains why cats don't bump into things the way we clumsy humans do.

Playtime!

One of the great pleasures of keeping a cat is its playful nature. For kittens, play is their schoolwork. Rough-and-tumbles with litter mates teach cat manners. Stalking Mum's tail or 'killing' a toy teaches hunting skills. Mad chases round the furniture are P.E. lessons! Cats never outgrow this playfulness. Adult cats play to keep fit – and also just for the fun of it.

Toys
Playthings range from a scrap of screwed-up paper to designer toys from pet shops. Moving objects, thrown or dangled on a string, always appeal. Make sure toys are safe. A ball of wool may be irresistible, but it can be dangerous to a kitten who swallows a length or catches a claw. Check stuffed toys such as catnip mice to make sure their eyes, ears and tails are secure and can't be swallowed.

Faithful retriever
We don't usually expect cats to play a game of 'Fetch' like dogs. But some, such as the wild-looking Abyssinian, thoroughly enjoy retrieving a ball. If your cat is one of these breeds, you'll probably be worn out before it is!

Make time in your day to play with your cat. Joining in its games helps to strengthen the bond between you.

Quieter cats often prefer hunting games, stalking a toy (or your dressing-gown cord) and pouncing on it. You can add to the excitement by making the toy move like real prey!

Kittens' play is enchanting to watch – and to join in with. But it's also serious business. Chasing a small, moving toy is practice for mouse-work later.

The destroyer
Foreign cats such as Burmese need a lot of entertaining. Like small children, they can cause absolute mayhem if they're left to amuse themselves. And scolding won't help them understand that torn curtains are their fault. It will just upset them – they were only playing! If you own a highly-active cat, provide lots of exercise to use up their energy.

Water sports
Swimming isn't a common cat pastime, but the Turkish Van is renowned for it. This cat takes its name from Lake Van in southeast Turkey, where it originates from. Known as the 'swimming cat', even the Van kitten apparently enjoys splashing about.

Very active cats (especially Foreign breeds like Siamese and Burmese) enjoy games which involve climbing, jumping and racing about. These are solo games, but sofas and curtains can suffer during these mad dashes, so you may want to distract them to play with a toy! Team games for cats tend to focus on play-fighting, and kittens have to learn to control their teeth and claws when tackling thinner human skin.

Body beautiful

In the wild, cats that don't keep fit starve. Even though domestic cats have trained humans to look after them now, they still take great care of their health. They take regular exercise and indulge in plenty of long snoozes. They enjoy a balanced diet, and they try to keep themselves spotlessly clean – sometimes with a bit of help from their friends.

The cat's comb
The cat's tongue is a very special tool. If *you* licked a cat's fur, you would just make it wet! But when a cat licks its fur it is actually combing it. Its tongue is covered with tiny spines, which work just like the teeth on our combs to tease out tangles and remove dead hairs.

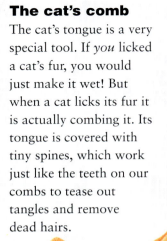

   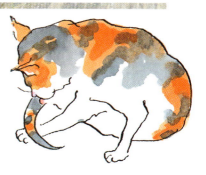

How to wash
Even a cat can't lick the top of its head! Instead, it wets its forepaw with its tongue to use as a flannel.

The cat can reach almost every part of its body. Underneath calls for a yoga position, with one leg in the air for balance.

The cat's neck turns further round than ours, so it can reach over its shoulder to wash. Bet you can't lick your back!

The small front teeth (the incisors) come in useful to nibble out grass seeds or tangles from the tail. And that's the job done.

Like us, cats need their beauty sleep – and here they are real experts. Cats spend two-thirds of their lives dozing! But instead of having a set bedtime, they curl up whenever they please, day or night.

If a sleeping cat is neatly curled up, it is just enjoying a catnap! In this light sleep its senses are still alert, and it can spring to full wakefulness in an instant. When it's in light sleep, the animal may drift into several minutes of deep sleep. During deep sleep, it uncurls its body to go completely floppy. You may also see it twitching, which means it's dreaming!

Cats can twist round to wash nearly every part of their body, but sometimes a friend will help. When cats wash each other, they are telling each other what good friends they are. They are also spreading their scent on each other, producing a shared 'family smell' – like a badge that says they belong to the same club! A human stroking a cat delivers the same message of friendship and belonging.

▲ *The Cat*, by Tsugouharu Foujita

Bringing up baby

Whether she has just one kitten, or more than a dozen (though it's usually four), the cat is a devoted mother. She chooses a safe, quiet nursery for her helpless babies, and hardly leaves them for the first couple of days. Once they start toddling about, she has her work cut out to keep them out of trouble.

1 Newborn
A gentle rubdown from Mum's tongue stirs the newborn kitten to start breathing. Its eyes and ears are sealed, but its nose is working – ready to locate the milk supply.

2 Mother's milk
Like all baby mammals, kittens need their mother's milk – and not just for its food value. The first milk she produces for them contains vital protection against disease.

Mother love
Kittens need a lot of care, protection and teaching. For eight weeks their mother is food supply, nurse, guardian, climbing frame and favourite plaything. It's hard work! Luckily, in real life she is likely to be more patient than the mother in this Victorian painting looks!

▲ *Playing With Mother*, by Horatio Cauldery

3 Carried away
A few days after the birth, the mother often carries her kittens to a new nest. It's a habit left over from the wild, where staying in one place for too long could attract the notice of predators.

Foster mum
Mother-love is so strong that cats may even adopt outsiders into a litter. Cats' foster-babies range from rats and puppies to zoo orphans such as marmosets!

▼ **Beauty the cat feeds Sammy the squirrel along with her own three kittens.**

Kittens are ready to leave home at between eight and twelve weeks. At this stage they are still babyish, and need special care from the new owner. This includes four small meals a day, lessons in cat manners and lots of attention. In the wild, they would stay with their mother until they could hunt like adults. Big cat species take longest to grow up. A tiger may stay with Mum for as long as four years!

6 Grown-up dinner
Kittens discover solid food at four to five weeks old, moving on to it gradually. At six to eight weeks, mother's milk comes off the menu completely.

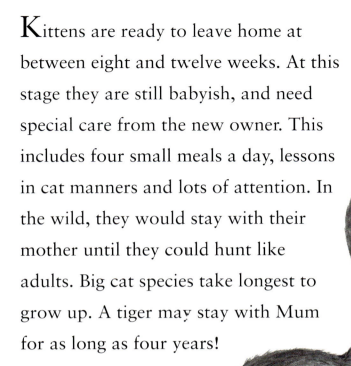

4 I spy...
Kittens' eyes start to open at between four and ten days old. It takes about three days for the eyes to open fully. Even so, their vision remains fuzzy for a couple of weeks.

5 Rough and tumble
Kittens start to toddle at about three weeks. A week later, they are steady on their feet and ready to learn the skill of washing themselves. They also discover how to play!

67

One legend tells how a cat earned the gratitude of Mary when it kept the Baby Jesus warm in the manger at Bethlehem. To this day, tabbies wear an 'M' for Mary on their foreheads – though a different legend links this mark with another cat-lover, the Prophet Mohammed.

Myth and magic

In Ancient Egypt cats were sacred animals and for centuries they remained linked with the supernatural. In the East, they were associated with both Buddha and Mohammed. In the West, medieval Christians connected them with the Devil. Superstitions link them with both good luck and bad, and they appear in folk tales as powerful, sometimes kindly magicians.

The witch's cat
No self-respecting witch would be without a cat! Around 1600, owning a pet cat could be enough to prove you a witch. With its glow-in-the-dark eyes, the cat was clearly magical. Some people thought it was the Devil in animal form.

Lucky charms
In the United States and many European countries, black cats are thought to be unlucky. But in Britain they bring good luck.

There are many myths and stories to explain how the cat was created. An Arabian legend describes how the cat's origins can be traced to the Flood. On board the Ark, Noah's pair of mice bred, and the vessel was soon overrun. When Noah asked the lion for help, the King of Beasts sneezed. Two miniature lions sprang out of his nostrils and set to work mousing – they were the very first cats!

To the Vikings, cats were the beasts of the love goddess Freya. In Norse legend, her chariot is drawn by two great cats, sometimes said to be wildcats or lynxes.

Breeders' handbook
Eastern cats inspired what is probably the world's oldest-surviving cat book, a scroll from medieval Siam (now Thailand). The *Cat Book Poems* describes, in words and pictures, the 17 kinds of cat then known. They include the ancestors of Siamese and Burmese, as well as the silver-blue Korat (below), said to have fur with "tips like clouds and roots like silver".

Early Siamese had a squint, and a bent tail – earned, legend says, in the course of duty long ago. While bathing, Thai princesses hung their rings on the cat's tail. He watched the rings so well he went cross-eyed, and he bent his tail by tying it in a knot for safety! In today's Siamese – except for feral ones in Thailand – squints and kinked tails have mostly disappeared.

Cats of the East

From Egypt, cats spread across the world. They were a great success in the East, making themselves at home in palaces and monasteries. It was here, centuries ago, that the first distinct breeds evolved, including the Siamese and Burmese.

Like their Egyptian ancestors, Eastern cats remained slender, leggy and long-headed. We still call cat breeds of this type Foreign or Oriental, classed apart from chunkier Western cats. They also differ in character, most being more active, more people-centred, and louder than other breeds!

Model 'Beckoning Cats' are good luck charms in Japan. They depict another ancient Eastern breed, the Japanese Bobtail, for centuries kept only by noblemen. This handsome stump-tailed cat is now popular outside its native land.

70

Cats of the West

The cat spread across Europe during the Roman Empire.

Egyptians might have called it a god, but practical Romans knew a good mouser when they saw one! Neither royal nor sacred, the Western cats had to work for their living. As pest control agents, however, they found a secure place in human homes – and then in human hearts. Today, most of our cats are loved pets rather than working breeds.

A new ingredient
Cats replaced tame mongooses as pest-controllers in Roman villas. They came in a choice of two colours. As well as the original tabby, blacks came on the scene in the first millennium BC.

Western cats started out as the same model as their Eastern relations. Paintings show us that European cats of the Middle Ages were still leggy and long-headed. But gradually they became stockier, with shorter legs and rounder heads. Modern European and American Shorthairs have a heavier build than their Oriental cousins – and pedigree British Shorthairs are the chunkiest of all. Perhaps due to their working ancestry, Western cats also have a more independent if less wilful character – which doesn't stop them making wonderful pets.

▲ A trio of 13th century ratters.

Tell no tails!
Originating on the Isle of Man, 'rumpy' Manx cats are famous for lacking tails. In fact, breeding (but not show) animals may have stubs ('rumpy-riser'), or short ('stumpy') or even full-length ('longy') tails.

▶ The lean American Shorthair is probably closest to ancestors of all the Western cats. Chunkier cats developed later. Recent creations include the Exotic Shorthair and the Scottish Fold.

American Shorthair
Leggier than the British, descended from the cats of 17th-century settlers.

British Shorthair
The pedigree version – much chunkier than non-pedigree pets.

Exotic Shorthair
Bred in the 1950s, this cat has some of the Persian's shape, but short hair.

Scottish Fold
A cat with unusual ears, which originated in Scotland in the 1960s.

73

Shaggy cat stories
Modern Persians (1) have an enormous coat. It's far too much for the cat to look after by itself, so don't even think of having one of these beautiful animals unless you have time for daily grooming. The Maine Coon (2) and Norwegian Forest Cat (3) are longhairs, but not of the Persian type. Their thick, shaggy coats are needed for cold winters. Both are working breeds and are perfectly capable of looking after their own coats.

The longhair story

The shorthair is the basic model of domestic cat. Longhairs first appeared in the East, and were introduced to Europe by travellers in the 16th century. These were slender, silky-coated Angora cats from Turkey. Later the rounder, fluffier Persian arrived from Persia (modern Iran). It was bred with other longhairs, including the Angora, which disappeared from the cat scene until recent times.

Luxury pets
An Italian, Pietro della Valle, is said to have brought some of Europe's first Angoras from Turkey in the 16th century. Described as "ash-coloured, dun and speckled, very beautiful to behold", they were soon in demand as luxury pets. Two centuries later, Persians were in and Angoras were out! The breed was revived in the 1960s – in two slightly different versions, American (from Turkish imports) and British (from long-coat Foreigns).

74

Heavily-coated Persians and silky Angoras have been joined by a wide range of other longhairs. Some, like the Birman and the Siberian Forest Cat, developed over centuries as distinct breeds in their own countries. Others are modern creations. Since the 1960s, breeders have produced a growing number of long-haired versions of popular shorthair breeds (see right). We now have a wide variety of coat lengths, but all these handsome cats need daily brushing to keep their coats clean and healthy.

The handsome Abyssinian now comes in a long-haired version, the Somali.

The Cymric is a long-haired Manx with a thick, woolly undercoat.

The Tiffanie is a long-haired cross between a Burmese and Chinchilla.

The Balinese is a long-haired Siamese. Some colours are called Javanese in the USA.

Cat shows

The first cat show, held in London in 1871, was a big event in cat history. It was organized by British cat-lover Harrison Weir to make more people appreciate their pets' beauty. It was a huge success, and the result was the 'invention' of the pedigree cat. Cats' appearance was no longer taken for granted, and suddenly there was a reason to develop distinct breeds. The first were created mainly by dividing existing types of cat by colour.

The first show

Cat breeds didn't really exist in 1871, so most classes were simply for different colours – mainly shorthairs. Even a Scottish wildcat was entered, but no one could coax it into a show pen!

At first, new kinds appeared by accident: a breeder spotted an unusual colour or coat type and decided to develop it. Later, new breeds were deliberately designed. A new breed has to be approved by show authorities, who must agree that it is genuinely different, worth adding to the collection, and has no health problems. If accepted, the new breed is shown on a trial basis for a while, until it is well established.

shape of tail

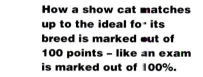

How a show cat matches up to the ideal for its breed is marked out of 100 points – like an exam is marked out of 100%.

shape of body, legs and paws

Shows today
Shows today are highly organized. The cats are usually kept safe in numbered pens, so that the judge cannot guess who owns them. At some shows, the pens are highly decorated and very individual; at these there is a separate judging area.

▶ Sorrel Abyssinian
New types may crop up in existing breeds. At first, Abyssinians only came in golden brown (Usual). Acceptance of the Sorrel opened the door for many more colour varieties.

Breeds continue to develop, but moggies still outnumber pedigree cats. All in all, the best cat in the world is your own, and even an alley cat is the descendant of the Egyptian gods!

◀ Peke-faced Persian
Its flat Peke-like face is a hit in the USA, but European cat-lovers find its runny eyes and snuffly breathing unacceptable.

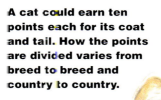

A cat could earn ten points each for its coat and tail. How the points are divided varies from breed to breed and country to country.

shape of head and ears

◀ American Curl
Some breeds appear by chance. The American Curl is descended from a curly-eared stray found by chance in California in 1981. This breed is not accepted outside the United States.

size, shape and colour of eyes

▼ Bengal
Breeders crossed domestic tabbies with wild leopard cats to create this beautiful new hybrid.

colour and condition of coat

WHAT TO LOOK FOR

clean ears

bright eyes

clean nose (a runny nose could indicate flu)

clean teeth and gums

clean, well cared-for fur, with no flea droppings

rounded body, not too thin or too fat (a pot belly suggests worms)

good temperament (nervous or aggressive kittens make poor pets)

plenty of bounce: a healthy kitten is alert and ready for fun

Choosing a cat

Your cat may be a member of your family for as long as 20 years, so it makes sense to choose carefully! Look for a healthy, active animal with a friendly attitude to ensure a good start. Male or female are equally good pets when neutered. Either a kitten or an adult cat may suit you. Kittens are irresistible but have much to learn, like house-training and claw control. Adults are usually better-behaved, but need time to settle in a new home.

A good start

A caring breeder will produce healthy kittens. Check that the mother cat has been well tended and the kittens are used to people. The breeder should have wormed the kittens, and should not allow them to leave home too young – they should be at least eight weeks old.

One or two?

If your kitten will be left alone all day, it may be kinder to have two, to keep each other company. But an only cat will be perfectly happy so long as its needs are met. Two kittens may be twice as much fun – but also twice the cost in neutering, vaccinations and food.

78

Pedigree breeds

If you are considering getting a pedigree, take the time to learn about the breed first. It's true that cat breeds vary less than dog breeds. There are no real giants or miniatures, though a Ragdoll (one of the biggest breeds) may weigh five times as much as a tiny Singapura. Most breeds have the same basic shape, but vary from slender to chunky. Compare the Siamese (long legs, body and head) with the Persian (short legs, body and face).

There are two main considerations when choosing a pedigree. First, do you have time to groom your cat every day? Daily de-tangling is essential for a longhair. Shorthairs, on the other hand, have easy-care coats. The one thing that varies hugely between pedigree breeds is temperament. Persians and Ragdolls tend to be laid-back and very relaxed. The Singapura is rather shy, while the Siamese is notoriously loud and attention-seeking.

Pet-shop kittens

Kittens in a pet shop window are tempting, but it's safer and kinder to collect your kitten direct from its breeder. Caring breeders don't sell to pet shops. A stay in a pet shop between homes is unsettling for a baby animal, and exposes it to a wide range of germs.

Rescue cats

It can be very rewarding to adopt a homeless cat from a rescue society. These charities normally check out the health and character of cats before re-housing them, and go to some trouble to match animals with suitable owners. They usually make a small charge.

The common moggy (or non-pedigree cat) is the basic model, or recipe, of cat. Taking this recipe as a starting point, pedigrees have been bred to emphasise particular ingredients of appearance and character. Special features such as really long fur, pointed markings or brilliant blue eyes are unlikely to appear in non-pedigrees. But both pedigrees and moggies offer a rainbow variety of colours and characters. Whichever cat or kitten you choose will make an equally lovable companion.

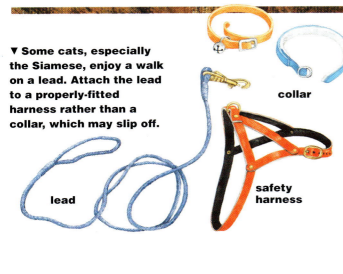

▼ Some cats, especially the Siamese, enjoy a walk on a lead. Attach the lead to a properly-fitted harness rather than a collar, which may slip off.

collar

lead

safety harness

Cat kit

Pet shops sell a bewildering variety of gear for cats. Don't worry, you won't need all of it! Some things you can do without and some you can make yourself: an old, soft towel makes a comfy bed, and the insides of toilet rolls are always popular toys. If your cat is to live indoors, it will have some special needs. For instance, a scratching post for its claws and a pot of grass to help keep it healthy.

In a flap
A flap fitted in a door will allow your cat to pop in and out as it chooses. It saves all that miaowing on the doorstep!

▼ Outdoor cats nibble grass, which helps them digest their dinners. Indoor cats needn't miss out: grow a pot of grass on a windowsill for them.

scratching post

grass

flea spray

comb

toys

brush and comb

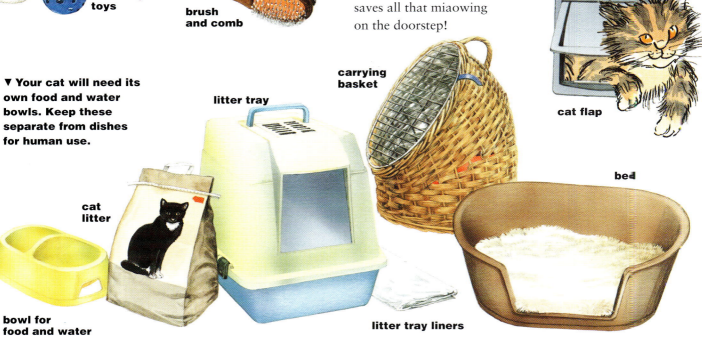

▼ Your cat will need its own food and water bowls. Keep these separate from dishes for human use.

bowl for food and water

cat litter

litter tray

carrying basket

cat flap

bed

litter tray liners

80

▲ A collar with an address tag may save your pet if it strays. Be sure to choose a safety collar, which has an elastic strip, so that if it catches on a branch your cat can wriggle free.

Cat carriage

Suitable carriers come in plastic, fibreglass, cane or even strong cardboard. You will need a carrying basket to ensure your cat's safety on trips to the vet (or anywhere else). It's not a good idea for your pet to associate the basket only with going to the vet! Get the basket out at other times too and let your cat get used to it.

▼ Claws need a regular work-out, and providing a scratching post may save the furniture! A platform on top means the post can do double duty as a climbing frame and activity centre.

Indoor toilet

A litter tray is a must for kittens and adult cats that are kept indoors. Keep it in a quiet corner, not too near your pet's food bowl. Trays can be open or covered – a cover gives your pet more privacy and helps to contain the smell! Even so, it will need cleaning every day. It's a good idea to check what type of litter a new kitten has been used to, as a sudden change may confuse it.

LITTER
1 fuller's earth
2 chalk
3 wood chips

litter scoop

Sleep easy

Pet shops stock a wide range of cat beds, from open plastic baskets to furry igloos. Some cats prefer to find their own bed – or to share yours! Wherever your cat sleeps, its bedding will need regular washing, and flea checks.

Cat care

Your cat's health depends on regular, well-balanced meals. Adult cats should be fed twice a day and will almost certainly remind you when it's mealtime! Growing kittens need several smaller meals a day, to suit their smaller stomachs.

If your cat is a longhair, remember to groom it daily. Shorthairs need brushing only once or twice a week to remove dead hairs. Grooming-time is also when you will spot any injuries, early signs of illness, or fleas. Best of all, it helps you to bond with your cat, which will enjoy the attention.

▲ *The Cat,* by Fernando Botero

Fat cat

A fat cat is not a healthy cat. If your cat is overweight, ask your vet for advice on a slimming diet. It could be that you are overfeeding your cat, or your cat may be tricking your neighbours into supplying extra meals! Like humans, some cats put on weight because they have a lazy lifestyle. Indoor cats especially need plenty of play.

A healthy diet

Cats need cat food! Dog food or household scraps don't contain the high level of animal protein they need – and even milk upsets many cats' stomachs. For a healthy diet, choose either canned cat food, fresh meat or cooked fish. Make sure there's always fresh water, too.

For a cat whose tail gets in the cream, breakfast and bathtime come together! Most cats love a lick of cream but it should only be given as an occasional treat.

Grooming matters

Grooming is more than beauty care. Longhairs depend on daily brushing to prevent tangles which, if neglected, may need to be clipped out by the vet.

Brush the fur gently, without tugging. Go against the way it naturally lies, lifting the fur upwards and outwards so that you work right to the roots. A comb is useful for lifting out dead hair.

Finish off the cat's face fur and neck ruffs with a smaller brush. An old toothbrush is ideal for this fine work – but please don't borrow one from the bathroom!

Great balls of fur

Loose hairs get swallowed when a cat licks its coat, and can build up in the stomach. There's no need to worry unless your pet can't get rid of its fur balls. If you spot the danger signs of a dry cough and loss of appetite, head for the vet. But remember, prevention is better than cure: regular brushing means fewer dead hairs for your cat to swallow.

Plant peril

Cats often enjoy nibbling plants, but some of these may be poisonous. Keep house plants out of reach – and provide a supply of grass for safe nibbles.

POISONOUS PLANTS
1 ivy
2 poinsettia
3 philodendron
4 caladium
5 laurel

Make sure that curiosity doesn't kill your cat by checking the house for dangers. Tuck electrical wires out of the way where they can't be chewed, and remember to put away poisonous household chemicals such as bleach. With a new cat or kitten, it's a good idea to protect your home as well, by moving breakable ornaments and house plants.

83

Understanding your cat

Cats can't speak our language, and we can't speak Cat. But that won't stop your pet telling you its needs, wishes and opinions in its own way. And, with a little patience, you can learn to treat the cats you meet politely – in their terms.

▲ George Adamson with Boy, one of the lions he rescued from zoo imprisonment in 1965.

Lion's share

When we make the effort to understand a cat, it will respond with affection – even if it happens to be a member of the big cat group. The film *Born Free* tells the story of the friendship between Joy and George Adamson and the lions who shared their lives. Here George and his 'best-friend' lion, Boy, enjoy a walk through the African bush.

One way to a cat's heart is through its stomach! By providing food you are telling your cat that you are its friend. But there's more to friendship than cupboard love. Cats need affection, too – and will give plenty in return.

Making friends

When visitors come, cats always seem to make a beeline for the one person who doesn't like cats. This should tell you how to approach a strange cat: don't! Cats don't like pushy people, so sit back, wait patiently, and let Puss make the first move.

Don't stare! It's not polite – and in cat language, it's a threat. Look slightly away, or try a couple of slow blinks to say, "I mean no harm."

To a cat, you're huge – so make yourself smaller, and less scary, by crouching down. Hold out one hand to invite Puss to come and investigate.

After a sniff, the cat will rub its head against your hand if it's ready for a gentle stroke.

Breeds of cat

Pedigrees are considered by some to be the aristocrats of the cat world. It is little more than a century since Harrison Weir 'invented' the pedigree cat, yet today there are nearly one hundred breeds. Thirty of these are longhaired breeds and the rest are shorthaired. Shorthairs can be split into two groups, depending on their body shape: chunky (Western) or slender (Eastern).

Some pedigrees come in just one colour – the Havana is only ever brown and the Bombay is always black. But the Persian, for example, can be one of over one hundred different shades and patterns!

Just to add to the confusion, two breeds share the same name! One Turkish Van (the 'classic') still lives by Lake Van in its native Turkey; the other has been bred in the West.

LONGHAIRS
1 Persian
2 Colourpoint Persian
3 Maine Coon
4 Norwegian Forest Cat
5 Ragdoll
6 Balinese
7 Somali
8 Birman
9 Cymric
10 Angora
11 American Curl
12 Turkish Van
13 Turkish Van (classic)
14 Tiffanie

Glossary

agouti A speckled 'salt-and-pepper' ground colour; seen in Abyssinians and between the dark bands of a tabby.

albino White with red eyes; a rare colour in cats.

AOC Any Other Colour (a show class).

AOV Any Other Variety (a show class for cats and dogs).

apple-headed

apple-headed A dog that has a high, domed forehead.

Asian Cat of Burmese type but with a different coat colour or length, for example Burmilla, Burmoiré and Tiffanie.

assistance dog Dog trained to help its disabled owner with everyday tasks, such as opening doors.

awn hairs Rather short, bristly hairs; the middle layer of a cat's coat.

barrel-chested Dog that has a large, rounded, projecting ribcage.

bay Howling call of a hound when hunting.

bench Open-fronted shelf where dogs are secured between classes at some shows.

bi-colour White with bold patches of colour. Show cats must have an even pattern of patches.

binocular With two eyes.

bird dog Dog used for hunting birds.

bitch A female dog.

bite How the top and bottom teeth of a dog fit together when the mouth is shut.

blanket Large patch of colour over the back and sides of a dog.

blaze Broad white stripe running down the face between the eyes; seen for example, in Tortoiseshell-and-Whites.

bloodline A cat or dog's family history.

bloodline

blue Grey colouring ranging from slate-grey to pale, bluish grey.

brace Two dogs of the same breed.

break A marked dent in the bridge of the nose, just below the eyes. Also called a stop.

breed Class of cats or dogs with similar appearance and related ancestry, for example St Bernard or Persian.

brindle Colour produced by bands of darker hairs on a lighter background, giving a stripy effect, as in Great Danes.

brindling A random mixture of hairs of different colours in a cat's coat (usually a show fault).

broken-coated A dog with wire- or rough-haired fur.

brush Tail of a long-haired cat.

cameo A cat that has white hairs with red, cream or tortoiseshell tips.

canine To do with dogs.

canines (1) The long, sharp teeth near the front of the mouth, used for catching and killing prey. (2) Members of the dog family.

brush

carnassials Ridged, sharp-edged teeth at the back of the mouth, used for gripping and tearing food.

carnivore Animal that eats meat. Cats and dogs are carnivores.

castration Neutering a male by surgical removal of the testes.

cat foot Tight, rounded foot.

catnip Mint-like garden plant irresistible to many cats.

cattery (1) Place where cats are looked after in their owners' absence. (2) Place where cats are bred.

cobby Stocky, short-bodied, short-legged and compact.

catnip

condition The state of a cat or dog's health, fitness and grooming.

conformation Body shape and size, characteristic of a breed.

corded A dog that has a long coat which naturally twines into separate, ribbon-like cords. Seen in Komondors.

coursing Hunting game with sighthounds.

corded

cropping Surgically removing part of a dog's ear to make the remainder stand up. This is illegal in the UK, but is still practised in parts of Europe and parts of the US.

cross-breeding Mating two different breeds or varieties together.

cur (1) A mongrel. (2) In some areas, a working sheepdog.

dam A mother cat or dog.

dapple Fur that has dark, irregular markings on a lighter background, as in some Dachshunds.

dew claw Claw on the inside of the foreleg, rather like a thumb.

dewlap Loose skin hanging in folds beneath a dog's throat, as in Bloodhounds.

dilute Paler version of a basic colour, such as blue, cream or lilac.

docking To amputate all or part of a dog's tail. This is illegal in the UK, but practised in some countries.

domestic Animals kept as pets.

double coat Coat with weatherproof top layer and soft, thick undercoat. The underlying awn hairs are the same length as the top layer of guard hairs.

down hairs Short, fine hairs; the bottom layer of a cat's coat.

double coat

drag Scent trail laid by dragging a strong-smelling lure, later to be followed by hounds.

dudley nose Dog's pink or light-coloured nose.

entire Not neutered.

evolution The process by which animals and plants develop and change over thousands of years.

feathering Fringes of long hair on a dog's belly, ears, backs of legs and tail.

feline To do with cats.

feral Domestic cat or dog that has gone wild.

flehmen Lipcurling expression made when air is drawn into the Jacobsen's organ.

flews A dog's long, overhanging upper lips, as in Bloodhounds.

flush To drive game from vegetation.

Foreign Cat breeds with long bodies, fine bones and wedge-shaped heads. Also called Oriental cats.

frill The ruff of fur around a longhaired cat's face.

fur ball Hair swallowed by cats while grooming, usually coughed up.

furnishings Long hair on the head, legs or tail of a dog required by certain breed standards.

gauntlets White 'socks' extending partly up the legs of cats, for example on the hind legs of Birmans.

gazehound Hound which hunts largely by sight.

ghost markings Faint, tabby markings sometimes seen in self-coloured cats, especially in kittens.

gloves White paws below dark legs of cats, for example on the forepaws of Birmans.

grizzled Bluish-grey colour of a dog's coat created by a mixture of black and white hairs.

guard hairs Long, straight hairs; the top layer of a cat or dog's coat.

guide dog Dog trained to lead a person who is blind.

hackles A dog's neck hairs which stand up in fear or anger.

hackney action Moving with forelegs raised markedly high.

hard-mouthed Dog that is over-rough with retrieved game or objects, marking it with teeth.

hare foot A dog's long, narrow foot, as in Tibetan Spaniels.

harlequin White with black or blue patches, as in Great Danes.

hearing dog Dog trained to alert its deaf owner to important sounds, such as alarm clocks and doorbells.

heat Time when a bitch is ready to mate.

hound marked White fur with black and tan patches; colour pattern typical of hounds.

inbreeding Breeding closely related cats or dogs (such as a brother and sister) together.

incisors Small front teeth, used for nibbling, tearing food and for grooming.

Jacobsen's organ Special sense organ in the roof of a cat's mouth, which 'tastes' scents in the air.

jowls Hanging fleshy lips, seen in Bulldogs and toms.

kennel (1) House for a dog. (2) Boarding house or breeding place for dogs.

kink Bend in the tail (a show fault).

kitten Cat under nine months old.

leather (1) Ear flap in dogs. (2) Bare skin of nose around the nostrils.

lilac Pale, pinkish-grey colour.

line-breeding Breeding together cats and dogs which are distantly (but not closely related).

litter Kittens or puppies born at the same time to the same mother.

litter tray Toilet tray for indoor use by domestic cats.

liver Reddish-brown-grey colour.

locket White patch under the chin of cats.

longhair cat Cat that has long fur, with no awn hair.

lurcher Hunting dog produced by crossing a gazehound with another working breed.

mask A face darker than the rest of the cat, as in Siamese.

merle Mottled or marbled colour formed by a mixture of hair colours.

mitts White paws in cats, extending further than gloves, but not so far as gauntlets, as in Mitted Ragdolls.

moggy Non-pedigree cat.

molars Large chewing teeth at the back of the mouth next to premolars.

mongrel Dog of mixed breeds that does not have a pedigree.

monocular With one eye.

neuter (1) To make an animal incapable of breeding by surgical removal of its reproductive organs. (2) A castrated male or spayed female animal.

nictitating membrane Film at the inner corner of each eye, which extends across the eye when the cat or dog is ill. Also called haw and 'third eyelid'.

odd-eyed Cat that has two eyes of different colours.

outcross To breed unrelated cats or dogs together.

overshot A dog that has an upper jaw that is longer than the lower, so top teeth extend past lower ones.

pack (1) A social unit of wolves and wild dogs. (2) A number of hounds kept for hunting.

pads Leathery skin on the soles of paws.

parasite Animal or plant that gets its food by living on or inside another living thing. Fleas and roundworm are parasites.

particolour White and another colour in roughly equal amounts.

pedigree (1) Pure-bred cat or dog whose birth has been registered with an official cat or dog club or kennel. (2) Document listing names of the last three to five generations of a cat or dog's ancestors.

pen Display cage in which a show cat stays when it is not being judged.

pencilling Delicate markings like pencil lines on the face of a tabby cat.

pied White with largish patches of colour.

point Rigid position in which some dogs freeze when they scent game.

pointed A cat that has points of a darker colour than the rest of the body, as in Siamese cats.

points A cat's ears, muzzle, tail and feet.

prefix Registered name of a breeding cattery or kennel, attached to the name of each kitten or puppy born there.

premolars Large chewing teeth situated between the canines and molars.

points

puppy Dog under 12 months old.

queen Female cat.

quick Vein and nerves in a cat or dog's claw.

rangy Long-bodied and long-legged cat.

recognition Official acceptance of a breed for show purposes.

registration Recording a puppy or kitten's birth and parentage with an official kennel, dog or cat club.

rex A cat that has a short, curly coat without guard hairs.

roan Having coloured and white hairs mixed together.

rumpy A Manx cat with no trace of a tail.

rumpy-riser A Manx cat with a tiny stub of tail.

sable Having black hairs lying over a lighter background colour.

self Having a coat of one colour. Also called solid and self-coloured.

shaded Having a coat of pale hairs which gradually darken towards the tips.

shell Having a coat of pale hairs which are coloured at the very tips.

show Showcase of cats and dogs (pedigrees as well as moggies and mongrels). The animals are judged according to a standard of points and the winners are awarded prizes.

sire A father cat or dog.

smoke Having a coat of dark hairs which are pale at the base.

sniffer dog Dog that is trained to find things, such as drugs or people, by smell.

soft-mouthed Dog that is able to retrieve objects undamaged.

sire

spaying Neutering a female by surgical removal of the ovaries and uterus.

species Group of animals or plants that are alike in some way.

spraying Marking territory with urine, usually by entire males.

squint Eye deformity, giving a cross-eyed look; sometimes found in Siamese cats.

standard of points Blueprint by which show cats or dogs are judged.

stern Tail of a hound or other sporting breed of dog.

stud (1) Tom cat kept for breeding. (2) Cattery.

stumpy A Manx cat with a short tail (instead of no tail at all).

ticked (1) Dogs with speckled fur with tiny spots of darker colour throughout. (2) Having each hair banded in two or three colours, as seen in Abyssinian cats.

tipped Hair that is a different colour at the end, as seen in Chinchilla cats.

stumpy

tom Male cat.

tortoiseshell A three-coloured cat, usually black, red and cream, but dilute versions exist, such as Blue and Lilac.

tricolour A three-coloured dog, usually with black, tan and white fur.

tipped

type Physical appearance of a cat or dog (or breed) in relation to the breed standard.

undercoat Short, woolly fur, under the top hairs, made up of awn hairs and down hairs.

undershot Dog that has a longer lower jaw than its upper, so that its bottom teeth extend past the upper ones.

usual Original colour of a cat breed, before varieties developed.

variant Cat bred from two pedigrees which differs from the breed standard and so cannot enter a championship at shows.

variety Colour form within a breed.

vibrissae Whiskers on a cat's head and wrists, adapted to sense what they touch.

wall eye Dog's eye that has a whitish or bluish iris.

whip tail Long, thin tail of a cat that tapers to a point at the end; as seen in Foreign Whites.

wild dog Wild species of the dog family, such as the Dingo or the African Hunting Dog.

wrinkle Loose folds of skin on the body or, more commonly, on the head of a dog.

wrinkle

Useful websites

The Cat Fanciers' Association
www.cfainc.org

Cats Protection
www.cats.org.uk

21 Cats
www.21cats.org

Support Dogs Charity
www.support-dogs.org.uk

The Kennel Club
www.the-kennel-club.org.uk

A kid's guide to dogs care
www.geocites.com/~kidsanddogs

RSPCA
www.rspca.org.uk

Famous cats and dogs

Airedale Jack
A World War I messenger dog that saved a British battalion. Cut off under heavy fire, they sent him to HQ with a message asking for reinforcements. Despite appalling wounds, he made the 6.5km journey, dying of his injuries as soon as he had achieved his mission.

Andy
Andy fell from his home on the 16th floor of a skyscraper in the 1970s, living to tell the tale. He holds the record for the longest, non-fatal fall in cat history.

Antis
A German Shepherd dog that flew with the Czech Air Force and RAF in World War II. He saved lives by detecting the approach of enemy aircraft, rescuing people from a bombed house and saving his master's life.

Barry
The most famous of Switzerland's St Bernard Hospice mountain rescue dogs, 1800-1812. He saved over 40 lives.

Beerbohm
London's longest serving theatre cat. For 20 years, Beerbohm was the live-in mouser at what is now called The Gielgud Theatre. Every so often, he would wander on stage during performances and upstage the actors, much to the delight of the audience.

Bobbie of Oregon
In 1923, Bobbie the dog was separated from his family while on holiday, and they were forced to leave him behind. He returned home to Oregon from Indiana in the USA. During the 4,800km, six-month journey, he crossed three rivers, the Great Plains and the Rocky Mountains.

Bothie
This terrier mascot of the Transglobe Expedition (1979-82) travelled 83,200km around the globe. The only dog to go to North and South Poles.

Brownie
In 1963, Brownie became one of the richest cats in the world after inheriting $415,000 when its American owner died.

Buddy
'First lady of the Seeing Eye', this German Shepherd was the first US guide dog (1920s). Her success kickstarted the guide dog movement in England and the USA.

Dragon
Dragon's master, Aubry of Montdidier, was murdered in 1371, and the dog's subsequent attack on Richard of Macaire was taken as an accusation. This led to the only case of ordeal by combat between man and dog – Dragon won and Macaire confessed to the murder.

Hachiko
Japan's answer to Greyfriars Bobby. After his master's death at work in 1925, Hachiko the dog waited for his train every evening for the next ten years. He became a national hero.

Hodge
The pampered cat of Dr Samuel Johnson (1709-1784), the renowned English writer. Dr Johnson was so devoted to his pet that he is reputed to have bought fresh oysters for him every day.

Laika
The first space traveller, launched in Sputnik II (1957). Although she was known as Laika, this is actually the dog breed name. As there was no means of bringing her back, she was doomed to die in space. In 1998, scientists published a formal apology for sacrificing her life.

Pickles
A mongrel which found the stolen World Cup in 1966 after Britain's top policemen failed to do so. Pickles became an overnight celebrity.

Socks
Socks is the much-loved black-and-white cat who belonged to Bill Clinton, US president 1993-2001. Socks was so popular with the public during Clinton's office, that he is reported to have received 75,000 letters and parcels a week from fans.

Sugar
When his owners moved to Oklahoma in the USA and left him behind, Sugar the cat embarked on a 2,400km journey to be reunited with them. His travels took 14 months to complete.

Towser
A great mouser. This tortoiseshell cat lived in Glenturret Distillery in Scotland and is reputed to have killed three mice a day throughout her adult life. All in all, this means that Towser killed approximately 29,000 mice before she died of old age in 1987.

Trixie
Trixie's master, the third Earl of Southampton, was imprisoned in the Tower of London during Queen Elizabeth I's reign. Missing her owner, Trixie the cat crossed London and entered his cell via the chimney. She kept the Earl company until he was released two years later.

Index

A
Abyssinian Cat 62, 75, 77, 87
Adamson, Joy *and* George 84
Afghan Hound 14, 15, 16
African Hunting Dog 9
African wildcat 48
aggression 41
agility training 43
Airedale Jack 91
Akita 45
Alaskan Malamute 45
American Cocker Spaniel 15
American Curl Cat 77, 86
American Indian Dog 11
American Shorthair 73, 87
American Wirehair Cat 57, 87
Ancient Egypt *see* Egypt, Ancient
Andy 91
Angora 74, 86
Antis 91
Anubis 33
Arctic Fox 9
Argos 34
art 50, 52, 65, 66, 82
Arthur, King 35
assistance dog 28
Australian Cattle Dog 25
awn hair 56, 57, 90
Aztecs 32

B
balancing 52-53
Balinese Cat 75, 86
Barry 91
Basenji 11, 15
Basset Hound 15, 44
Bat-eared Fox 9, 17
Beagle 20
Bearded Collie 25
Beauty 22
'Beckoning Cats' 70
bed 38, 80, 81
Beerbohm 91
Belgian Shepherd Dog 45
Bengal Cat 77
Bichon Frise 45
Birman 75, 86
black cat 69, 72
Black Shorthair Cat 59
Black-and-Tan Coonhound 44
black-footed cat 48
Blitz 22
Bloodhound 17
Bobbie of Oregon 91
Bobcat 48
Bobtail 70, 87
body (dog) 12-13
Bombay Cat 86, 87
bone *see* skeleton
Border Collie 17, 22, 24
Border Terrier 14
Born Free 84
Botero, Fernando 82
Bothie 91
Bouvier des Flandres 26
Boxer 37
Bracco Italiano 23
breed 44-45, 76, 79, 86-87, 88
breeding *see* cat breeding
Briard 15, 45
British Shorthair 73, 87
Brittany Spaniel 23
Brownie 91
Buddha 68
Buddhism 33
Buddy 91
Bull Terrier 15, 44
Bulldog 12, 13, 15, 45
Bullmastiff 45
Burmese Cat 63, 70, 75, 87
Burmilla 87

C
Cairn Terrier 21
canine 49, 54, 88
carnivore 48, 60, 88
carrying basket 80, 81
Cat Book Poems 70
cat breeding 70, 78
cat, choosing 78-79
cat family 46-47
cat flap 80
catnap 65
cattle dog 24, 25
Cauldery, Horatio 66
Cavalier King Charles Spaniel 30, 45
Cavall 35
Cave Lion 49
Celts 27
Cerberus 32
Chartreux 87
Cheetah 48, 55
Chihuahua 30, 33
Chinchilla 59, 75
Chinese Crested Dog 15
choke chain 38
Christian legend 32, 68
Civet 48
claw 52, 54-55, 80, 81
climbing 52-53, 54
Clouded Leopard 46, 47
coat *see* fur
Cocker Spaniel *see* English Cocker Spaniel
collar 38, 80, 81
Collie 15, 17, 22, 24, 25
colour 56, 76, 79
colour-blindness 58
communication 40-41, 84-85
Coonhound 44
Corgi 25, 45
Cornish Rex 57, 87
Cougar 51
Coyote 11
Curly-coated Retriever 15
Cymric 75, 86
Cynodictus 6

D

Dachshund 12, 20, 44
Dali, Salvador 52
Dalmatian 15, 19, 45
Dawn Dog 6
della Valle, Pietro 74
Devon Rex 87
dew claw 55, 88
Dhole 5
diet *see* food
Dingo 9, 11, 25
Dinictis 48
Dire Wolf 7
Dobermann 14
dog, care of 38-39
dog, choosing 36-37
dog family 4-5
dog, language 40-41
down hair 56, 88
Dragon 91
dreaming 65

E

ear and hearing 15, 16, 18, 53, 60-61, 73, 78
early cat 48-49
early dog 6-7, 10-11
Eastern cat 70-71, 73, 86
Egypt, Ancient 33, 34, 68, 70
Egyptian Mau 87
Elkhound 15, 45
English Cocker Spaniel 44
European Shorthair 73, 87
evolution 48-49, 88
   see also early dog
Exotic Shorthair Cat 73, 87
eye and eyesight 16, 18, 53, 58-59, 67, 68, 78

F

facial expression (cat) 59
falling 52-53
Felis (little cat) 48, 49
feral cat 70, 89
fighting 54-55
Fishing Cat 55
Flat-coated Retriever 44
Flat-headed Cat 47
flea 38, 78, 80, 81, 82
Fo Dog 33
food 38-39, 54, 66, 67, 80, 82, 85
Foreign Cat 70, 74
foster-baby 67
Foujita, Tsugouharu 65
fox 7, 8, 9, 17
Fox Terrier 15, 44
Foxhound 21
Freya 69
fur (cat) 56-57, 64-65, 76, 78, 79
   see also longhair cat; shorthair cat
fur (dog) 14-15, 25, 39
fur ball 83, 89

G

Genet 48
German Shepherd Dog 15, 17, 22, 26
ghost dog 35
Golden Jackal *see* Jackal, Golden
Golden Retriever 23, 26, 29, 37
Gordon Setter 44
grass 80
Great Dane 19, 45
Greek legend 32, 34
Grey Wolf 7
Greyhound 11, 13, 44
grooming 39, 64-65, 74, 79, 80, 82, 83
guard hair 56, 57, 89
guarding 10, 26-27
guide dog 28-29
gundog 22, 23, 42, 44

H

Hachiko 91
hair *see* fur
Halsman, Philippe 52
harness 80
Havana 86, 87
haw, *see* nicitating membrane
health 64-65, 78, 80, 82-83
   see also vet
'hearing ear' dog 28
herding 24-25
Hesperocyon (Dawn Dog) 6
Hodge 91
homing instinct 60
hospital visiting dog 29
hound 14, 15, 16, 17, 20-21, 35, 44
Hounds of Hell 35
Hungarian Puli 14
Hungarian Vizsla 44
Huntaway 25
hunting (cat) 49, 53, 54, 58, 60, 61, 62
hunting (dog) 7, 8, 10, 11, 17, 20-21, 22
Husky 45
Hyena Dog 7

I

illness 82
incisor 54, 65, 89
Indian legend 34
indoor cat 80, 81, 82
Indra 34
Irish Setter 23
Irish Terrier 21
Irish Water Spaniel 15
Irish Wolfhound 44
Isis 34

J

Jackal, Golden 9
Jacobsen's organ 60, 89
Jagdterrier 21

Jaguar 48
Japanese Akita 45
Japanese Bobtail 70, 87
Javanese Cat *see* Balinese Cat
Jesus Christ 68
Jungle Cat 48

K
Katmir 32
'killing bite' 54
King Charles Spaniel 45
kink 70
kitten 62, 66-67, 78-79, 82, 83, 89
Komondor 26
Korat 70, 87

L
Labrador Dog 23, 29
Laika 91
lapdog 30
Lassie 25
lead 38, 80
Leopard 54, 77
Leopard Cat 46, 77
Lhasa Apso 45
Lion 49, 53, 69, 84
Lion Dog 33
litter tray 80, 81
longhair cat 57, 74-75, 79, 82, 83, 86
Löwchen 45
Lynx 48, 55, 58, 69

M
magic 34-35, 68-69
Maine Coon 59, 74, 86
Malamute 45
Maltese Dog 45
Maned Wolf 9
Manul 48
Manx Cat 73, 75, 87
marbled cat 46
Maremma 25
Margay 53

Mastiff 11, 12, 45
Mau 87
Medieval Times *see* Middle Ages
Mexican Hairless 5
Miacis 6, 48
Middle Ages 20, 26, 30, 73
milk 66
miniature dog 30
Miniature Poodle 30, 45
moggy 46, 79, 77, 89
Mohammed 68
Mongoose 48, 72
mongrel 36
moulting 57
mountain rescue *see* rescue dog
mousing 60, 69, 72
Munchkin 87
Muybridge, Eadward 50-51
myth 32-33, 68-69, 70

N
Neapolitan Mastiff 45
nest 66
neutering 78
New Zealand Huntaway 25
Newfoundland 45
nictitating membrane 59
night vision 59
Nile River 34
Noah's Ark 34, 69
Norfolk Terrier 15, 37
Norwegian Forest Cat 74, 86
Norwich Terrier 44
nose and sense of smell 60, 66, 78
Nottie 26

O
obedience 24, 43
Ocelot 48
Ocicat 87
odd-eyed cat 59, 89
Old English Sheepdog 37, 39
Old English White Terrier 44

Oriental Cat *see* Foreign Cat
Osiris 34
Osteoborus 7

P
pad 13, 89
painting *see* art
Pallas's cat 55
Panthera (big cat) 48
Papillon 30
Paresse 50
paw 52, 57
pedigree 57, 76, 79, 86-87, 89
Peke-faced Persian Cat 77
Pekingese 15, 16, 30, 33
Pembroke Welsh Corgi 25, 45
Persian Cat 57, 59, 74, 77, 79, 86
pet shop 79, 80
photograph 50-51
Pickles 91
play 18, 39, 41, 62-63, 67
Playing With Mother 66
Pointer 23
poisonous plant 83
Polish Lowland Sheepdog 25
Pomeranian 15
Poodle 45
Pug 12, 15, 30
Puli 14
puppy 18-19, 37, 38, 39, 42, 43, 90
'puppy farmer' 37
puppy walker 29
purring 47
Pyrenean Mountain Dog 15, 45

R
Raccoon Dog 6, 9
Ragdoll 79, 86
Red Fox 7, 9
rescue dog 29
rescue kennel 36
rescue society 79
Retriever 15, 23, 26, 29, 37, 44

roaring 47
Romans 27, 72-73
Rose Hill ghost dog *see* ghost dog
Rottweiler 26, 45
Rough Collie 25
running 12-13
Russian Blue 87

S
Sabre-tooth 48, 49
safety 83
St Bernard 22, 45
Saluki 20, 44
Samoyed 45
Sand Cat 57
scent 17, 22-23, 41, 56, 60
Schipperke 15
Scottish Fold Cat 73, 87
Scottish Terrier 44
scratching post 80, 81
search dog 23
search and rescue dog *see* rescue dog
'seeing eye' dog 28-29
senses 16-17, 58-61
Serval 61
Setter 23, 44
Seven Sleepers 32
Seychellois 87
Shar Pei 15
sheepdog 24-25, 37, 39, 45
Shepherd Dog 15, 17, 22, 26, 45
Shetland Sheepdog 25, 45
Shih Tzu 30
shorthair cat 57, 59, 73, 74, 75, 76, 79, 82, 86, 87
show 75-77
show dog 43
Siamese Cat 59, 70-71, 75, 79, 80, 87
Siberian Forest Cat 75
Siberian Husky 45
Singapura 79, 87

Sirius 34
'sixth sense' 60
skeleton 12-13, 50-51
skull 12, 54
Skye Terrier 21
sleeping 64, 65, 81
smell *see* nose; scent
Smilodon 49
Smooth Collie 25
Smooth Fox Terrier 44
Smooth-haired Dachshund 44
sniffer dog 22, 23
Snowshoe 87
social status 40
Socks 91
Somali Cat 57, 75, 86
Song Dog 11
Sooty 60
Sorrel Abyssinian Cat 77
spaniel 15, 16, 23, 44, 45
Sphynx (cat) 57, 87
sporting dog 44
squint 70
Steinlen, Théophile 50
Sugar 91
support dog 28-29
Swedish Valhund 25
swimming (cat) 63

T
tabby cat 68, 72, 77
tail 14-15, 41, 53, 73, 76, 77
taste, sense of 60
teeth 13, 49, 54-55, 65, 78
temperament 78, 79
terrier 14, 15, 19, 21, 37, 44
Tibetan Spaniel 45
Tiffanie 75, 86
Tiger 67
tongue 64, 65, 66
Tonkinese Cat 87
Towser 91
toy 39, 62, 63, 80
Toy Poodle 30
tracking 22

training 40, 42-43
Trixie 91
Turkish Van 63, 86

U
undercoat 56, 75, 90
usual (cat) 77, 90

V
vaccination 78
Valhund 25
vet 59
Viking 69
vision *see* eye and eyesight
Vizsla 44
Volpino 30

W
war dog 26, 27
washing 65, 67
Weir, Harrison 76
Welsh Hillman Herder 44
Welsh Terrier 21
West Highland White Terrier 14
Western cat 70, 72-73, 86
whisker 15, 57, 60, 61
wild dog 8-9, 11, 14
wildcat 49, 69, 76
Wire-haired Dachshund 20
Wire-haired Terrier 22
witch's cat 68
wolf 7, 8, 10-11, 12, 15, 24, 26, 44
wolfhound 44
working dog 45
worms 78

Y
Yorkshire Terrier 19

Acknowledgements

The publishers would like to thank the following
illustrators for their contributions to this book:

Andrew Beckett (illustration) 66-67; **Mick Brownfield** 4-5; **John Butler** 18, 52-53; **Vanessa Card** 6-7; **Jim Channel** (Bernard Thornton Artists) 47*br*, 48*tr*, 49, 53*tr*, 54*bl*, 57*mr*, 58*tr*, 59*tr*, 61*bl*, 63*ml*; **Paul Cox** 84-85; **Gino D'Achille** (Artists' Partners) 8, 22; **Peter Dennis** 26; **Sandra Doyle** 12-13, 51*br*, 54*tl*, 55*tr*; **Madeleine Floyd** 65*t*; **Lynda Gray** 58-59; **Ray Grinaway** 42, 43; **Martin Hargreaves** (Illustration) 46-47; **Sue Hellard** (The Organisation) 78*mr*, 79*ml*, 81, 83*m*, 85*r*; **Kate Hodges** 88-90; **Sally Holmes** 28-29; **Christian Hook** 24, 27, 86-87; **Ruth Lindsay** 11; **Ch'en Ling** 8; **Angus McBride** (Linden Artists) 10; **Malcolm McGregor** 11, 14-15, 20-21, 23, 25-26, 30, 37, 55*br*, 57*t*, 73*r*, 74*l*, 77*r*, 79*t*; **Tony McSweeney** 68*tl*; **Danuta Mayer** 20-21, 32-33, 34-35, 72-73, 74-75; **Clare Melinsky** 34, 35; **James Marsh** 71; **Karen Murray** 62-63; **Nicki Palin** 30, 31, 38; **Liz Pyle** 68-69; **Mike Rowe** (Wildlife Art Agency) 19, 40, 41, 54-55, 76-77, 78; **Claudia Saraceni** 5, 16-17, 60-61; **Paul Stagg** (Virgil Pomfret) 56-57, 82-83; **Mark Stewart** (Wildlife Art Agency) 36-37; **Eric Tenney** 50-51, 64-65; **Helen Ward** (Virgil Pomfret) 9, 14-15, 19, 23, 38, 39, 40; **Ann Winterbotham** 48*b*, 56*bl*, 80, 81*tr*, 82*br*, 83*bl*.

Marmaduke the Multifaceted Dog and Marmalade the Multifaceted Cat
by **Kate Hodges**
Decorative border (pages 46-87) by **Paul Stagg** (Virgil Pomfret Agency)

The publishers would also like to thank the following for
supplying photographs for this book:

Pages **9***br*: NHPA/Stephen Dalton; **11***bc*: Axel Poignant Archive/Roslyn Poinant; **17**: Concept @ Charles Barker (*cl*), Fotomas Index (*br*); **21***tr*: Bonhams/Bridgeman Art Library; **22***b*: Hulton Getty/Fred Morley; **23***cr*: Northamptonshire Police; **25**: Ronald Grant Archive (*tr*), Corbis/Paul A. Souders (*br*); **26***tr*: Express Newspapers; **30***cr*: Hulton Getty; **33***br*: Private Collection/Bridgeman Art Library; **36***bl*: RSPCA/Ken McKay; **41***cr*: RSPCA/Tim Sambrook; **49***t*: Paul Franklin; **50***bl*: British Museum – 'Paresse' from *Des Chats* Théophile Steinlen; **50-51, 68***br*, **76***bl*: Mary Evans Picture Library – *Animals in Motion* Eadward Muybridge (50-51); **52***m*: Magnum Photos – *Dali Atomicus* Philippe Halsman; **60***mr*: Dragon News & Picture Agency; **64***tr*: Liz Artindale; **65***br*: © ADAGP, Paris and DACS, London 2001/Bridgeman Art Library; **66***b*: Bridgeman Art Library – *Playing With Mother* Horatio Cauldery; **67***l*: Oxford Scientific Films; **69***t*: Retrograph Archive Collection; **70**: Roger Tabor (*tl*), Paul Sehault/Eye Ubiquitous (*r*); **73***tl*: British Library Ms. Harleian Bestiary; **77***tl*: Marc Henrie, Asc; **82***bl*: Marlborough Gallery, NY – *Cat* © Fernando Botero; **83***mr*: Nickleodeon Animation; **84***m*: Topham Picture Library.

Every effort has been made to trace the copyright holders of the photographs.
The publishers apologise for any unavoidable omissions.